A More Excellent Way

A Discussion of the Matter and Manner of Entire Sanctification

By

Howard W. Sweeten, Evangelist
Author of "Must We Sin?"

NAZARENE PUBLISHING HOUSE
2923 Troost Ave., Kansas City, Mo.

PREFACE

Every worthy or unworthy cause, and every system or organization with a purpose, has as a measuring line to its success, a definite objective. The intricate parts of a machine may be diversified in the manner of their operation; yet these parts all work in unison to a definite end. Anyone who has stopped long enough to observe the various qualities of nature, cannot help but be impressed with the fact that everywhere, there is to be seen the finger prints of intelligence and design, as well as the creative genius of the Master Mind.

The doctrines of Divine Revelation constitute the outstanding source of authority upon all questions relative to man's moral and spiritual integrity. A proper understanding of the doctrines of the Bible are essential, therefore, to practical and experimental Christianity. To say that it makes no difference what a man believes, so long as he is sincere, is the climax of absurdity. One might as well say that it makes no difference whether automobiles are constructed with lead parts, or steel, so long as the manufacturer is sincere in his belief that lead is as hard as steel; or one might say that it makes no difference whether a person eats digestive food or not, so long as he sincerely believes the food is all right; or one might say it makes no difference where he invests his money, whether his investments are safe or not, so long as he honestly has confidence in them. Error is just as disastrous to the soul who accepts it as truth, as it is to one who knows it is error.

It is as impossible to build Christian character without doctrinal knowledge as its basis, as it would be to erect a substantial building without adequate foundation. Practical religion is inseparable from doctrinal religion. Those who talk about the day of doctrinal preaching being a thing of the past, and who have much to say about a broad and latitudinous range of religious belief, are conspicuous for their lack of practical fruits. One writer says, "The duties of religion are inseparable from religious truth; and all its experimental realities are through the 'belief of the truth." The Holy Ghost always employs divine truth in the work of salvation. "Sanctify them, through thy *truth*," "If ye know the *truth*," "I am the way and *the truth*," and other like Scriptures confirm this fact.

It is not the purpose of the author of this volume to treat the subject in an exhaustive manner; neither is it his wish to make a display of scholarship, therefore, we have adhered strictly to the English translation of the Scriptures, and avoided delving into technical interpretations of Greek words and phrases, principally for two reasons. First: The readers of this book, for the most part, will have a decidedly limited knowledge of the Greek, and it is the desire of the writer to make the contents plain, rather than scholarly, in an effort to reach the masses as well as the classes. Second: Any person who would not be convinced in the light of the English translation, is in all probability so tainted with skepticism or prejudice, that while his scholarship may demand an exegesis of the Greek, his faith would not accept the interpretation. We are reminded upon the pages of Sacred Writ, that, "the common people heard him gladly," therefore, we prefer to make this a plain treatise, reduced to the maximum of simplicity, and within the range of the understanding of those who are not familiar with theology and theological terms. We must learn at the very threshold of Christian experience, that neither temporal blessing nor spiritual benefits can be definitely received from God through any other channel than that of faith, and so long as there is a question mark in our minds concerning such matters, we automatically disqualify ourselves to receive from the Divine Hand. We implore the reader therefore to give us an unprejudiced hearing, and not to form conclusions, until the evidence in the case has been heard and considered without prejudice.

If the great truth which is the subject matter of this volume is a Bible doctrine, then we must conserve it, and rescue it, as far as possible, from the abuses which have been heaped upon it by the prejudice of some and the ignorance of others. The hatred and prejudice which gather about it, through the misinformation of some, and the absurd and ridiculous conduct of others, is no excuse for its being ignored and neglected. "Christ on the cross," says one writer, "is still Christ, just as much as when he was the adoration of the multitudes. Gold is just as much gold when it is hidden in the ore, as when it has been separated from the base alloys; the alloys may hide its beauty and mar its lustre, but they cannot depreciate its value. Likewise, it is the business of Christian instructors to remove all the alloy, and base dross of prejudice, and misinformation, and present to the people their full privileges in Christian experience." The doctrine of full salvation should be preached truthfully, scripturally, and fearlessly, without depreciating the value of regeneration on the one hand, and the exciting fanaticism on the other.

It is the purpose of Satan, God's arch enemy, to poison as much as possible, every person who would otherwise give an unprejudiced consideration to religious truth; and especially, is this so, if that particular truth has any vital relation to Christian experience. Many have been deprived of the blessed privileges of the gospel, because they have allowed uninformed sources of information to prejudice them against the truth. One of Satan's favorite methods in misleading great numbers, is to point out to them some inconsistent individual, or some ridiculous person as an example of Christian experience. Let the reader not forget that God never does anything inconsistent nor ridiculous, and that any privilege that God may have provided for the human family at the price of the blood of His Son, is well worthy of our honest and serious consideration.

To what extent can a man be saved from sin in this world? Is salvation merely partial, or is it complete? Just how much can the Almighty do toward delivering a man from sin in this life? Is it possible for man to be saved from all sin while here below?

These are vital questions, and well worth our honest and sincere consideration. Many ministers and laymen throughout the church are convinced with Andrew Murray, "That there is a universal complaint of feebleness of the Christian life, and that there are tens of thousands of souls longing to know how to lead a better life. They find in God's Word, promises of perfect peace; of a faith that overcomes the world; of a joy that is unspeakable; of a life that is abiding in Christ, and hidden in the hollow of God's hand, and in the secret of His pavilion; but, alas! thousands are without it, and know not how to obtain it."

It is the sincere desire of the author of this book, that his endeavor to present to the reader a plain and scriptural treatise upon the subject of "A More Excellent Way," may be rewarded by its proving to be a blessing and source of inspiration to those who read it. With this desire, we send it forth into a world already crowded with books, praying God's blessing upon it, and the reader.

Yours for success,
HOWARD W. SWEETEN.

CONTENTS

Chapter		Page
	Preface	3
I	Is It Scriptural?	11
II	The Voice Of The Ecclesia	25
III	Diagnosing The Case	36
IV	The Standard	41
V	A Bit Of Misinformation	53
VI	What Is It?	62
VII	Suppression Or Eradication?	71
VIII	When Is It Obtained?	85
IX	The "Second Blessing"	110
X	How To Receive It	122
XI	A Human Being	141
XII	Why?	154
XIII	The Evidence	166
XIV	Catechetical Appendix	179

A MORE EXCELLENT WAY

CHAPTER I

Is It Scriptural?

In dealing with problems which have relation to the souls of men, and their spiritual needs, there is no clearer light to be found, nor any firmer ground upon which to stand, than that which is afforded by the "Thus saith the Lord." All Scripture is given by inspiration of God, and is profitable for doctrine, for reproof, for correction, for instruction in righteousness" (2 Tim. 3:16). It therefore does not *contain* the Word of inspiration; but it *is* the Word of inspiration itself, and consequently speaks with veracity and authority.

Psychologists, physiologists, biologists, scientists, and philosophers may speculate upon the mysteries of the soul, and discuss its nature, its qualities, and its endowments; but God passes the speculative and experimental stage, and by a complete diagnosis prescribes for humanity upon the basis of their needs as well as their deeds; in fact the plan of salvation and the whole redemptive scheme is based upon the decision of one who actually knows. His is the final word to be said upon the subject; and the word of Him who holds the destiny of us all in His hands, is the only authoritative and safe instruction in the matter of spiritual truth.   One ounce of divine revelation is worth a ton of scholastic speculation, when it comes to the intricate problems that pertain to the soul here, and its destiny hereafter.

The plan of salvation, and God's program in saving men, are not based upon the opinion of those who are in ecclesiastical authority, but upon the "I, the Lord, have spoken it."   For this reason we inquire into the teaching of the Scripture upon the subject matter of these pages.   "Thy word," says the Psalmist, "is a lamp unto my feet, and a light unto my path."   Therefore, in the light of this Word which speaks with authority, and whose wisdom upon soul problems is unexcelled, let us seek a knowledge of the truth.

That God has planned, and provided, a something, in the realms of spiritual possibilities that he calls sanctification, would hardly be denied, in the face of so many Scriptures which positively declare it to be the case, and in so many more that imply it.   When we read such Scriptures as Eph. 5:25, 27; 1 Thess. 4:3; 1 Cor. 1:30; John 17:17; 1 Thess. 5:23; Heb. 12:14; Heb. 13:12, 14; and many others of like significance, they ought to settle the matter, in the mind of any unprejudiced person, that there is in the range of spiritual possibility and attainment a gracious experience (whatever it may be) that God calls sanctification; something that God has made possible for us in Christ Jesus as indicated by 1 Cor. 1:30, "But of him are ye in Christ Jesus, who of God is made unto us wisdom, and righteousness, and *sanctification*, and redemption"; something that through Christ is the privilege of the Church, as implied by the apostle's language to the Ephesians (Eph. 5:25, 27). Something for which Jesus himself prayed earnestly for His disciples to receive, as may be seen from John 17:17, and in fact something to which all believers are entitled, as may be seen from the prayer of Jesus recorded in John 17:20. Something that was of sufficient importance to us, and interest to himself, that he would suffer humiliation, pain and even death to bring that something to pass. This is indicated by the statement of the apostle when he says, "Wherefore, Jesus also, that he might sanctify the people with his own blood, suffered without the gate." Who can read these texts and others equally as clear, without being impressed with the fact that there is some kind of sanctification which occupies a very large place in the program of God, and in the experience of men?

We shall not attempt to define the term as used in the Scriptures just here; whatever it means we will determine in another chapter. All we ask the reader to observe at this time is, that whatever it may be, it is the will of God, and is possible through the blood of Christ; it is the blood-bought privilege of the church, and the divine requisite for admission to heaven (Heb. 12:14, R. V.). The ministry of Jesus and His apostles was freighted with references to this matter. Jesus prayed for His disciples to be sanctified; the apostle Paul prayed for our sanctification, and declared that without it no man should see the Lord. With these references and many more, what should be the attitude of the professors of New Testament Christianity toward this question of sanctification? Can I ignore it? Can I afford to wrongly interpret it? What personal obligation do I have concerning this matter? If I do not understand the matter, or manner of sanctification, can I be content to remain in ignorance regarding the subject, when God has caused these things to be written for my edification? Can I take this negligent attitude toward the Word of God, and His will concerning me, and still remain in His favor? What bearing do these Scriptures have upon my own experience? How responsible am I concerning them? These and many other questions confront every honest and unprejudiced seeker after truth and light. It is not wisdom nor piety that causes men to disregard what God has been pleased to write for their edification and profit; and no frank and open minded person can disregard the statements of divine revelation upon this, or any other matter, which God has been pleased to write for our edification, without suffering irretrievable loss to the soul's best spiritual interests.

We believe it is right that we should make the Word of God the basis of our faith, and to recognize it as the one source of authority concerning matters of salvation. In his letter to the church at Corinth, the apostle Paul, after exhorting to a spirit of unity a church that was much divided among themselves, urges that each member shall have due respect for the other, and that each shall recognize the other's place and ministry in the great program of God. He then calls attention to the utter fallacy of making human wisdom the basis of truth. "Because the foolishness of God is wiser than men." It is a misfortune that is nothing short of a calamity for any person to discard his faith in God's Word, in order to substitute the wild speculations of scholastic bigotry. The need of the world today is not the conglomerated guesses of finite speculation, but words of wisdom and authority. No one but the rankest kind of critics who are infidel to the core will question the wisdom of Jesus Christ upon matters that have relation to our personal salvation. It was Jesus Christ that said, *"Sanctify them, through thy truth."* It was Jesus Christ that suffered without the gate that He might *sanctify the people* with His own blood. It was Jesus Christ that gave Himself for the Church, that He might *sanctify it,* and it would seem that this *sanctification* was to be the medium through which He was to present it to Himself a glorious Church, not having spot, or wrinkle, or any such thing; but that it should be *holy* and without blemish (Eph. 5:25, 27). These scriptural statements relative to the matter of sanctification ought therefore to settle the fact of its being scriptural.

The apostle Paul reminds us that in Jesus Christ we are to have wisdom, righteousness, sanctification and redemption. It is strange indeed to find those who will concede that in Christ we are to have wisdom, right-eousness and redemption, but who want to repudiate the possibility of our having sanctification. By what manner of interpretation can we accept three qualities of the text and repudiate the fourth? If we are to have wisdom, righteousness, and redemption, then surely we must also have sanctification.

If God's Word is to be the basis of our faith, and the authoritative source of our information upon the subject, it would seem that the plain statement, "This is the will of God, even your sanctification," ought to put the matter beyond controversy; for the phraseology of this text is such, if applied to any other subject in the Scriptures, it would put the matter beyond debate. Take, for instance, the question of the mode of water baptism. Perhaps there is no other subject about which there is so much discussion and so many varied ideas; yet if the Scriptures had said, this is the will of God that you be either sprinkled or immersed it would have put forever beyond the realm of controversy that much mooted question as to the method of administering water baptism. When the writer was first examined for license to preach, among other questions asked was the question concerning baptism. "Is immersion baptism?" asked the examiner. We answered, "The Methodist church accepts it as baptism." (We were being examined for preacher's license in this denomination.) "But," said the examiner, "is it baptism?" We replied, that inasmuch as we were being examined for a preacher in this church we would of course accept its position on this question. The examiner then reversed the question and asked, "Is sprinkling baptism?" We again responded with the same answer. In fact, we did not purpose to settle in a dogmatic manner a question upon which there has been so much debate, and on which so many opinions have been expressed. However, if the Scriptures had used the same phraseology in reference to baptism that it has on this matter of sanctification, it would have been very easily answered, for the plain statement, "This is the will of God," would have settled the matter and put it forever beyond the realm of controversy. The Scriptures do not say *this is the will of God* that you be immersed or sprinkled, but it does say exactly this thing relative to sanctification; and we believe that the will of God ought to be the will of every true Christian. Their attitude should always be, "Thy will be done."

Whatever is the will of God most certainly ought to be the will of every one of His sincere children. To know God's will and disregard it; to be informed as to what God's will is concerning one and deliberately dodge it; to have a conception of the divine will and ignore it, will certainly, sooner or later, disqualify one from remaining any longer in divine favor; for "How can two walk together unless they be agreed?" asks the prophet. To know that "This is the will of God, even your sanctification," and never seek to have a definite understanding of the matter, nor make any effort to obtain it, and remain utterly indifferent to it, is to put a question mark in the minds of all who know the facts, concerning your sincerity. Why pray, "Thy will be done," and then make every effort possible to free moral agency to defeat your own prayer by your negligence and apathy regarding the matter? Why say, "Thy will be done" in our lives, if we are unwilling to make any effort or sacrifice to have it so? Does the reader pray "Thy will be done"? Does he desire it to be done? Jesus says, "What things soever ye desire, when ye pray, believe that ye receive them, and ye·shall have them." The fact that we are exhorted to pray for it, and the fact that it is in harmony with God's will, is sufficient evidence that this is within the realm of spiritual possibility. "This is the will of God, even your sanctification." Reader, it is God's will; is it yours? According to Bible teaching, sanctification is the will of God, and in His remarkable Sermon on the Mount, Jesus taught His disciples to pray, "Thy will be done," therefore, we may have the experience of sanctification while in this life, or Jesus is guilty of the colossal blunder of teaching us to pray for that which can never be obtained, and uttering prayers that can never be answered.

The fact that sanctification is the will of God, is prima facie evidence that it is His desire. Should the writer will to the reader a sum of money; at the settling of his estate the administrator would certainly see that the proper cash or properties were surrendered to the beneficiary. There must, however, be a death before the will can be executed; hence, Jesus died in order to execute the will as is seen from Heb. 13:12, "Wherefore Jesus also, that he might sanctify the people with his own blood, suffered without the gate." In fact, the Savior declares that this is exactly what He came into the world to do. "Then said he, Lo, I come to do thy will, O God. . . . *By the which will we are sanctified through the offering of the body of Jesus Christ once for all.*" These scriptures and others of like quality give evidence that provision has been made for the execution of the Father's will, which includes our sanctification.

Now it sometimes happens that when there is a member of the family of the deceased that has been left out of the will, he will often seek to contest the will and have it broken, and thus defeat the purpose of the one who made the will. We must not overlook the fact, therefore, that Satan, who was once a member of God's great family, but cast out and rejected, is now doing his utmost to defeat the purpose of this will of God. If there is any one benefit of grace that is peculiarly detested and opposed by Satan, God's arch enemy, it is this matter of our sanctification. He is doing his utmost to defeat the purpose of God, and to prevent His will being executed in the hearts of men. He seeks to prejudice every person against this wonderful experience, or to convince them that it is beyond the possibility of attainment in this life.

The outstanding hatred of Satan to God's will and his untiring effort to defeat it; his determination to deprive God's children of their blood bought inheritance, (Acts 26:18) and rob them of their privileges in this world, explain to a large extent the special prejudice existing toward the doctrine of full salvation. Suppose that those who are professedly followers of Christ should ridicule and antagonize the doctrine of regeneration, or ignore it as they do the doctrine of sanctification; would we not say that they were defeating the purpose of God who has declared, "Ye must be born again"? Would we consider such persons in divine favor who thus opposed the purpose of

God? Yet there seem to be many who can repudiate
and ignore the Word of God in regard to the matter of
their sanctification, who have no obligation nor responsibility whatsoever concerning the will of God.
The mystery to the writer is how such persons can disregard their duty relative to the truth and keep in
favor with God. Many seem to think they are doing
God's service to dodge and repudiate the doctrine and
experience of sanctification, when in fact four times
as much is written relative to this matter as is recorded
concerning justification. Surely Satan is still in the
business of deception, and the attitude of antagonism
and unbelief to this, or any other fundamental doctrine
of the Christian religion, is the same old sophistry of
hell that was manifest in the Garden of Eden. "God
hath said, Ye shall not eat of it, neither shall ye touch
it, *lest ye die*." But Satan replies, "Ye shall not surely
die." It is the same old policy of deception, an effort
to disregard God's will and set our own in opposition
to the will of the great and good God. Yea, hath God
said, "This is the will of God, even your sanctification." Is it yours? Are you giving the lie to God's
declaration by declaring it is not for you? If our wills
are set in opposition to God's will, and we are full of
antagonism and unbelief relative to this matter, we are
doing nothing less than practicing the same old sophistry of the Garden of Eden. How can the reader be
with God in some matters and with Satan in some?
No man can serve two masters. One thing is certain.
Satan is opposed to anything that is God's will, and
when one opposes God's will he has most assuredly

arrayed himself against God and identified himself with the forces of Satan, whose business it is to, in every way, defeat the purpose of the Almighty. Think, reader, think! How can two walk together unless they be agreed? If God agrees to your sanctification, and you do not agree to it, how can you walk together? If God says, "He hath not called us to uncleanness, but unto holiness," what right has any teacher of the Scriptures to discount this statement and seek to interpret it otherwise? If God says, "Follow peace with all men, and *the sanctification,* without which no man shall see the Lord" (R. V.) what right has any teacher to assume that we can see God without this sanctification? Surely a doctrine of such grave importance is worthy of sincere and earnest investigation, and it may pay the reader to accept the statements of the Word of God at face value, rather than making the opinions of popular divines the basis of the possibilities of religious experience. When God says, "Without holiness no man shall see the Lord;" why should we go about to discourage any attempt to measure up to this standard, and call it fanaticism, or false and hurtful teaching? If Beelzebub were here himself, he could not invent a more brazen and impudent bit of infidelity with which to defeat God's Word and purpose, than is being faithfully and vigorously propagated in many modern pulpits. "Marvel not," says the apostle, "if Satan be transformed into an angel of light, and *his ministers* as the ministers of righteousness." Here we see that Satan's ministers represent themselves as the ministers of righteousness, and we doubt not that his most valuable assets in the ministry are those who pose as God's ministers, but who in fact neglect and antagonize those scriptural doctrines which are not palatable to their way of thinking. We are tempted to say that if it were not for the great number of pulpit incumbents in this country, the cause of God might thrive and prosper to a much greater advantage. How easy it is to find upon the pages of Holy Writ exhortations, advice and even commandments concerning this matter; but alas! how easy it is to find ministers, who ought to know better, exhorting the people not to believe such dangerous heresy, and to beware of such fanaticism. Alas! that such infidelity should have crept into the pulpit, and put a question mark in the minds of the constituency of the church against God's truth. Methinks Martin Luther was not far wrong when he said, "If the clergy could have destroyed the Church of Jesus Christ, doubtless it would have been destroyed long ago."

In discussing the scripturalness of the doctrine of sanctification, may we call the attention of the reader, in passing, to the prayer of the apostle Paul as recorded in 1 Thess. 5:23. Here he is praying for the God of peace to sanctify us wholly (that is entirely) and preserve us blameless unto the coming of the Lord Jesus Christ. Is the apostle committing a blunder in praying for our sanctification? Is he foolish and beside himself? Has he drifted into fanaticism and unsafe and dangerous teaching? We are informed that "all scripture is given by inspiration." If so, this prayer is the product of inspiration. Is the apostle made to pray, by the Holy Ghost, a foolish and fanatical prayer; one that can never be answered and is doctrinally in error? If so, he might as well pray for us to become cherubims, or seraphims, or archangels, as to pray for us to be sanctified. The reader will do well to use discretion in his criticism and opposition to those who advocate the doctrine of sanctification; for if the minister is a fool or a fanatic for preaching what has been written, and is in doctrinal error, then the apostle is in the same predicament for writing such extravagant language; and what about the Holy Spirit who inspired it? If this prayer is only visionary and can never be answered, what a mistake on the part of Divine Wisdom to inspire such language. If it is fanatical and doctrinally in error, what a blunder on the part of Almighty God to so misdirect the apostle in his writing on this point. What a calamity that God did not have some of our modernistic intellectuals (?) to direct Him in the matter of what should have been written.

Beloved, we have no selfish ends to serve, no ax to grind, no favors to ask, no blind devotion to any particular phraseology, and no desire to force men to adopt our particular "shibboleth"; we are not contentious for terms (though we do think that Bible phraseology is preferable), nor the manner of presenting them; but we are dogmatic in our conviction that there is a gracious doctrine and experience revealed in the Word of God, which He calls sanctification; and that this experience may be obtained by faith, through our Lord Jesus Christ, as a present privilege. It is furthermore our conviction that it is an indispensable requirement, as a fitness for citizenship in heaven, and the glorious privilege of seeing the Lord.

Shall we believe what we like, and base our faith altogether upon what learned divines have to say regarding the subject; or shall we take the Word of God at face value? Great and learned divines may give us much truth but they may also give us some error. As one writer puts it, "Creeds and standard authors may be true exponents of Bible doctrine, but only so far as they harmonize with the Word of God can they be relied upon to direct us safely in our investigation of truth." Hence we ask concerning this doctrine, "Is it scriptural?"

CHAPTER II

The Voice of the Ecclesia

This is an age of intellectualism, an age of learning; one that boasts of its scholastic achievements; when marked progress and rapid strides of advancement are being made in all branches of learning. The printed page is perhaps the outstanding means of properly informing the public in these various realms of investigation. Every branch of science, every fraternal society, every line of mercantile business, have their printed organs by which to inform their constituency, and thus promote the highest quality of efficiency and success among their followers. Radio corporations, moving picture industries, labor organizations and even churches find this the most feasible plan to inform and rightly instruct their followers. The churches, therefore, through the printed page of doctrinal statement seek to inform and edify their communicants as to the articles of their faith; by such publications as catechisms, confessions of faith, manuals, disciplines and various statements of doctrine. A church without a creed, as some profess to be, is a church that believes nothing, and usually stands for about the same thing. A church creed is merely a statement of what they believe, and is for the purpose of letting the public know of the things for which they doctrinally stand.

25

In this day of advanced scholarship, it is surprising to see how many communicants there are in the various denominations that are utterly incapable of giving an intelligent statement of the doctrine of the church of their choice; many, in fact, are so far from knowing the doctrine of their church that should they hear it, they would take offense, and consider it unsound and fanatical teaching. Especially is this so concerning the doctrine of sanctification, which constitutes the subject matter of these pages. The attitude of the ministry of the Protestant churches upon the matter of sanctification is generally to pass it up as a dangerous doctrine, that leads into fanaticism; and to generally ignore it. It may be that the silence of the pulpit upon the subject is largely responsible for the amount of misunderstanding regarding the matter; this silence having left the impression that either they are opposed to it, or that it is of such minor importance as to hardly be worthy of consideration; or that it has no place in the doctrine of their denomination. Doubtless the reader, if he is even a casual observer, knows there is a marked silence in most pulpits upon the subject of sanctification. Just how, or what, can cause a man to neglect a subject that has such a prominent place in the Scriptures, and such vital relation to personal experience in the things of grace, is difficult to answer; especially when that particular theme is one of the fundamental articles of their religious doctrine.

When we assert that all orthodox churches, Protestant and evangelical, believe in, and have incorporated in their declarations of faith and creedal statements, this gracious doctrine and experience of sanctification; we believe that we are fully sustained by their catechisms and other doctrinal and authoritative statements which confirm it. May we observe a few of the leading Protestant denominations upon the matter.

The Methodist Episcopal Church and the Methodist Episcopal Church South, which are the two outstanding branches of Methodism, and which form, perhaps, the largest Protestant denomination in the world, are very clear upon the subject of sanctification. By the direction of their general conferences of 1900 and 1902 respectively, committees were appointed by the bishops of the churches to prepare a new catechism (statement of doctrine) to be used by both churches. It is stated in the preface of this catechism, which bears the title, "The Standard Catechism," and is published by the Methodist Book Concern, of Cincinnati and New York, that it is prepared for older people, in distinction from their junior catechism, and that it forms a complete course of catechetical instruction for the communicants of that great ecclesiastical body. On page 39 of this Standard Catechism, question 126 is asked as follows: "What is Entire Sanctification or Christian Perfection?" Answer: "It is that attainable grace in which the believer, having been made free from the guilt and bondage of sin in justification, and from the death in sin by regeneration, becomes a servant of God and has his fruit unto holiness; the inward conflict between the flesh and spirit is finally overcome, so that duty becomes privilege, and God's child loves

Him with all his heart and mind and soul and strength, and his neighbor as himself."

If English language can convey any significance whatever, we have here a plain statement of the fact that entire sanctification is that *attainable grace for the believer, who has been made free from the guilt of sin in justification, and the death in sin by regeneration;* that is, having been pardoned, and quickened, or made alive spiritually, they may now receive an attainable grace; which is to be the remedy for the inward struggle between the flesh and spirit; and which is to produce fruit unto holiness. Lest the reader may be inclined to think that this is an unsafe or unsound doctrine which we are teaching; we would have you note further what is said concerning this catechism, which teaches this strange (?) doctrine. Under the head, "Episcopal Approval," and above the signatures of the bishops there appears the following, "The catechism now presented to the Methodist people of the whole country, having been approved by the bishops of the Methodist Episcopal church, and the Methodist Episcopal church, South, *is hereby commended as a safe manual of Christian doctrine.*" If, therefore, the great Methodist church endorses this doctrine of sanctification for believers, justified, and regenerated, it is certainly acknowledging that this work of grace is subsequent to regeneration (for it could not be otherwise if it is for justified and regenerated believers) and that it is the privilege of those who have come to know Jesus Christ as their personal Savior. It would seem, therefore, to be the height of inconsistency for a minister or layman of this denomination to make any objection whatsoever to its being taught in their pulpits, when the ecclesiastical authority of their church has declared it to be, "*a safe manual of Christian doctrine*." In the answering of this question No. 126, they hereby concede that there is an *attainable grace* for the believer who is justified and regenerated, called sanctification. It would be difficult to make the matter any clearer than this. If this is safe doctrine according to the declaration of the Methodist bishops, and conforms to the creedal statement of this great ecclesiastical body; if it is the doctrine which gives us our fruit unto holiness; without which no man shall see the Lord, (Heb. 12:14), and if it is the privilege of those who have been justified and regenerated to attain it; why the protracted silence on the part of some, and the bold antagonism on the part of others to such instruction? Why?

It may also interest the reader to know what that great ecclesiastical body known as Baptists have to say regarding sanctification. As we are writing these lines, there is upon the table before us a Baptist catechism, published by the American Baptist Publication Society, of Philadelphia, Pa. According to the preface of this catechism, it is called the "Prize Catechism," because it was the result of a $300 prize, which was offered for the best and most concise statement of Baptist doctrine. The writer of this catechism was the winner of that prize; hence we conclude that the judges awarding the prize for this work, considered and endorsed its contents as being a good and a safe state-

ment of Baptist doctrine, to be followed by the communicants of that grand old ecclesiastical organization.
On page 14 of this catechism, question 37 is asked,
"What is sanctification?   Answer: Sanctification is
the *work of the Holy Spirit in the regenerated soul, by
which it is made holy.*" In giving this statement of
doctrine they cite the following scriptures, as a basis
of authority for such doctrinal declaration: 1 Thess.
5:23; 2 Cor. 7:1; Heb. 12:14. Who could give a
clearer exegesis of any doctrine than that which is here
given of sanctification?   Three things stand out on the
surface of this statement that leave no question in the
mind of the reader as to what is being said, and as to
what the attitude of this great body is toward the
matter of defining sanctification. (1) It is the work
of the Holy Spirit. (2) It is for the regenerated soul.
(3) The purpose of this work is to make the soul holy.
This is not merely the opinion of one isolated writer
upon the subject; but this declaration has passed in-
spection by authoritative Baptist theologians, and been
rewarded a prize of $300 for its brevity and accuracy,
and it might be of interest to the reader to know that
this catechism was met with such favor on the part of
Baptists that, according to a prefatory statement, a
number of editions were published totaling many
thousands of copies, for the safe doctrinal instruction
of the communicants of that great church. Surely a
doctrine so clearly stated as this ought not to leave any
doubt in the minds of the communicants or friends of
this denomination as to what their attitude should be
upon this point. Whether the doctrine of sanctifica-

tion is vigorously and aggressively promoted, or whether it is sadly and shamefully neglected, changes not the church's position upon this matter, it only advertises the faithlessness or ignorance of the minister upon a subject that is vital to Christian experience.

We cannot understand why ministers of any denomination which has this great doctrine of sanctification as a part of their creed should refrain from preaching and teaching the doctrines of their own church. We venture, however, to surmise that it might be one of the following reasons. (1) That it would be too embarrassing to preach to others a higher standard of integrity than the preacher himself enjoyed; and would be somewhat embarrassing to exhort others to an experience which he himself did not possess. Such inconsistency might result in a boomerang effect of having to face the problem of "Physician, heal thyself." (2) It may be due to the fact that they have been so engrossed with the social program of their church that they have failed to obey the scriptural injunction, "Study to show thyself approved unto God, a workman that needeth not to be ashamed, *rightly dividing the word of truth.*" This may result in his not being properly indoctrinated in the theology of his own denomination. This is often the case in regard to laymen and we believe it is possible in the case of the minister also. (3) It may be due to the fact that though they know the doctrine of their church, they are aware of the fact that there is a peculiar reproach that accompanies this matter of sanctification (Heb. 13:13), and their desire to be popular and to have a pull with certain classes, causes them to refrain from a type of preaching that would sound the death knell to carnality, and the many selfish and social indulgences that would not be consistent with a sanctified life. There is no doubt but that truth is often sacrificed for the sake of popularity. Regardless of the attitude, however, of the clergy upon the doctrine and experience of sanctification; upon investigation it will always be found that there is incorporated in the articles of their religion an experience subsequent to regeneration called sanctification.

It is now time to let another voice be heard. In the Westminster Shorter Catechism, the Presbyterians ask a number of questions relative to Christian experience, among which are the following: Page 9, Question 31, "What is effectual calling?" Answer, "Effectual calling is the work of God's Spirit, whereby convincing us of our sin and misery, enlightening our minds in the knowledge of Christ, and renewing our wills, He doth persuade and *enable us to embrace Jesus Christ,* freely offered to us in the gospel." Effectual calling, therefore, *doth enable us to embrace Jesus Christ,* according to Presbyterian doctrine; and we take it that anyone who has embraced Jesus Christ has become a Christian. Now question 32 asks, "What benefits do they that are effectually called partake of in this life?" Answer, "They that are effectually called *do in this life* partake of justification, adoption, *sanctification,* and the several benefits which, in *this life* do either accompany or flow from them." Here is a statement to the effect that sanctification is one of the benefits, which is the privilege of those who have embraced

Jesus Christ, and that such privilege is to be enjoyed *in this life.* If the reader is interested to know just what their interpretation of that sanctification might be, we quote further. On page 10, question 35 is asked, "What is sanctification?" Answer, "Sanctification is the *work of God's free grace, whereby we are renewed in the whole man after the image of God.*" In other words, according to Presbyterian doctrine, sanctification is the work of God's grace: the purpose of which is to renew us in the whole man, after the image of God; and this sanctification, or renewing after the whole image of God, is for those who have been effectually called, and embraced Jesus Christ, and is to be received and enjoyed in this life. A doctrine so clearly stated, and so important in its relation to personal experience as to renew us in the whole man after the image of God, should be widely and vigorously propagated, and especially if that image consists in that holiness without which no man shall see the Lord. May God raise up Presbyterians that will spread scriptural holiness to the ends of the earth.

Let us turn our attention now to another religious body to further confirm our statement that sanctification is incorporated in the articles of religion of all evangelical Protestant denominations. We will travel now to Dayton, Ohio, where the publishing interests of the United Brethren church are located. Here is published the United Brethren Hand Book. The preface to this doctrinal statement well says, "An intelligent understanding of the character of the religious denomination to which one belongs is important. In a church like the United Brethren in Christ, in which the members so fully direct the policy and methods, all, even the youngest, should be instructed in its history and work, its principles and government. . . . To those who have no access to more extended books, who desire in a brief space an outline of the work and history of the denomination, this little book is offered with the hope that, in a part at least, it will meet their wants." Under the heading of "Confession of Faith" on page 19, article 11, "of sanctification," we read, "We believe that sanctification is the work of God's grace, through the Word and the Spirit, *by which those who have been born again* are separated in their acts, words and thoughts from sin, and are enabled to live unto God, and to follow holiness, without which no man shall see the Lord." Here we are right back again tramping over the same old theological ground. Sanctification the work of God's grace, for those who have been born again, for the purpose of giving men that holiness, without which no man shall see the Lord.

It does seem to the writer after such clear statements and general agreement upon this matter, of all denominations, that we ought not to be so divided upon the matter; but should press this truth home to the hearts of our people everywhere, until they would be made to feel their need of that holiness, without which no man shall see the Lord; that holiness which is the divine requisite for a happy and harmonious dwelling place with God forever.

The Church of the Nazarene is a comparatively young ecclesiastical body; it has grown so rapidly since its organization, however, that it is now nearing 100,000 communicants. In their manual of doctrine of government, they have this to say relative to sanctification: Page 24, 25.

"Entire sanctification is that act of God, subsequent to conversion, by which regenerate believers are made free from inbred sin, and brought into the state of entire devotement to God, and the holy obedience of love made perfect. It is provided for, through the precious blood of Jesus, and is wrought instantaneously by the baptism with the Holy Spirit; the conditions being entire consecration and appropriating faith, and to this work and state of grace the Holy Spirit bears witness." This covers the ground and makes the matter of the attitude of the Church of the Nazarene clear beyond controversy; and we would say of it, as Mr. Wesley said of Methodists, that God has raised them up for the purpose of furthering this doctrine and experience.

If the foregoing pages of this chapter have not made it clear to the mind of the reader that this is the doctrine of most, if not all, of the Protestant denominations, it would be a hopeless task to continue the discussion any further. If we have herein spoken the truth, why should we be afraid to promote an experience of religion that is so universally acknowledged by all? Why call that unsound and unsafe, which is conceded to be a safe manual of Christian doctrine for evangelical Protestantism?

CHAPTER III

Diagnosing the Case

The matter of salvation is based upon man's needs, as well as his deeds. He who has gone to infinite expense in providing the great redemptive plan has not failed to accurately diagnose our malady and provide accordingly.

It would be a foolish physician that would walk up to the door of the hospital, throw a bushel basket of prescriptions in the door, and say to the head nurse, "Give these out among the patients." It would be the height of folly for any physician to undertake to prescribe for his patients until he had first diagnosed their condition. Let the reader never think that God has made the ridiculous blunder of providing a plan of salvation, that has cost Him the blood of His dear Son, without first making a clear diagnosis of the subjects' need. If the immortal soul's destiny is dependent upon the plan of redemption, which the Almighty has provided, and if He has made an accurate diagnosis of our condition and prescribed accordingly, it is imperative that we should know the nature of our malady and the provision or remedy which Infinite Wisdom has decreed shall meet our need.

Says the Rev. Jesse T. Peck, D. D., "The choice of God for the moral condition of the human race was perfect purity; hence He created man in His own image. As this was once the choice of God, it must be eternally so; and the divine preference or will can never be met but by perfect moral purity. Sin interfered with this choice, to the full extent of its existence and reign, and hence called out the severest divine displeasure. As man by becoming a sinner has incurred the divine displeasure, he can be saved from calamity and made perfectly happy only by entire deliverance from sin. The sacrificial offering of Christ and the means and appliances of the gospel reveal the plan of salvation as being for the purpose of destroying sin and the restoration of man to the image of God. Remedial measures originating in God must aim directly at the destruction of sin."

If this is accomplished, the nature of the malady is such that it will require justification and sanctification to morally restore man to the image of God. This is due to the fact that a diagnosis of the case reveals the twofold nature of sin, calling for a twofold remedy. Every Bible student is aware of this theological fact concerning sin. (1) There is actual sin. (2) There is inherent sin. Actual sin has to do with our actions, sustains a relation only to our conduct; it can be forgiven. Inherent sin has to do with our condition rather than our conduct, and is of such a nature that heaven's brightest pardon could not meet its needs. Actual sin is forgiven; inherent sin is cleansed; whether both these needs are met in one master stroke of the Great Physician, or whether each kind of sin is dealt with separately, constituting two epochal events in Christian experience, we will discuss in a later chapter. We are only trying to show here that the very nature of our malady is such as to require both pardon and purity, justification and sanctification. One writer says, relative to this matter, "I wish to emphasize a basic truth, that guilt and corruption are not correlative terms. Guilt implies transgression, corruption implies condition; guilt relates to effect, corruption relates to cause; guilt deals with individual responsibility, corruption is engendered of another; guilt requires pardon, corruption requires cleansing or purification." This manner is not out of harmony with the accepted teaching of orthodoxy. The Methodist Episcopal church says, (Standard Catechism, page 36, question 114) in answer to the question, "What is sin?" "It is any violation of God's law, or any lack of conformity thereto." Here we have the two kinds of sin, any violation (actual) and lack of conformity (inbred). Presbyterians say, "Sin is any want of conformity unto, or transgression of, the law of God." Here again we have the same twofold expression concerning sin, transgression of, or conformity to. A diagnosis of the malady therefore reveals the fact that our moral affliction is twofold in its very nature, and must, therefore, have a twofold remedy to meet the need; hence pardon for transgression, purity or cleansing for inherent sin. It will require both pardon and cleansing to restore us to the image of God.

Let us carry the diagnosis a step farther. We have called the reader's attention to the nature of the malady; now let us examine the patient and determine what effect this malady has had upon him. Man is a complex being. With reference to his personality, he is one; with reference to his substance, he is two, material and spiritual; with reference to his nature he is three, body, soul and spirit. Here is a wonderful creature that is a unit, a dichotomy and trichotomy. Using scriptural terms, however, we will say he is a trichotomy, and we are to deal with body, soul and spirit. Each one of these elements in a man's nature has suffered as a result of the fall. The spirit, or spiritual quality in man, is dead, dormant and inactive; hence God always represents the sinner as being dead in trespasses and in sins. We know that he is not physically dead, but spiritually; therefore the apostle says, "You who were dead, hath he quickened." The soul, the next quality in man's nature, is diseased or depraved, and just as the spirit must be quickened and brought out of the tomb of spiritual death into newness of spiritual life, so the defiled soul must be cleansed by obeying the truth through the spirit. The body in the fulness of time will also be redeemed by resurrection transfiguration, with all that this implies. Here, then, is regeneration for the spirit, sanctification for the soul, and glorification for the body. Yes, thank God! In the fulness of time this mortal shall put on immortality, and we shall stand before the King, who has washed us in his own blood; and shall join in the glad song, "Unto him that loved us, and washed us from our sins in his own blood . . . to him be glory and dominion forever and ever."

The apostle Paul says, "Wherefore he is able to save them to the uttermost that come unto God by him,

seeing he ever liveth to make intercession for them."
If this statement is true, and he is able to save to the
uttermost, then he must provide for any deficiency that
sin has produced in human nature. In order to do this,
we must be made alive (born again), must be cleansed
(sanctified) and in the fulness of time this mortal shall
put on immortality (glorified).

The reader may rest assured that a clear diagnosis
has been made concerning man's need, and that provision, ample and sufficient, has been made to restore
him to the divine image through regeneration, sanctification, and ultimately glorification.

The twofold nature of sin it would seem, therefore,
necessitates the twofold work of pardon and purity,
and the threefold nature of man calls for regeneration,
sanctification and glorification.

CHAPTER IV

The Standard

Everywhere in the realms of creation can be seen manifestations of the fact that the God who designed all things is a God of purpose and system. On every hand may be seen the fingerprints of intent and design, and marked evidences of the Almighty's purpose. Nowhere is this more manifest than in the plan of salvation. The forethought of God for man seems to have been that of holiness. Before the foundation of the world, it was decreed that man "should be holy and without blame, before him, in love." It is very evident that the matter of holiness was not a second or after-thought with God. When He made man He made him holy (in the divine image) and the whole purpose and plan of salvation is to restore to man that lost estate, and give to him again the divine image of righteousness and true holiness. If man is to ever enjoy the friendship of his Maker and bask in His smile of approbation, it must be because He which hath called you to holiness has been pleased to know that you have heard and responded, and have not only been forgiven of your sins, but have been cleansed from all sin.

Many scriptures such as Eph. 4:1, 1 Thess. 4:7, 5:23,24, 1 Peter 1:15, Heb. 12:14, and others of like significance, seem to signify that God's standard of

New Testament Christianity is that of holy character and life. If the purpose of the plan of redemption is to restore men to their lost state (image of God,) then to lower the standard below a life of holiness would be to defeat the very objective of the entire plan of salvation. It would further seem that if God had chosen us in Him before the foundation of the world that we should be holy, and had called us to it, and planned to make us so, we would be utterly without excuse if we fail to avail ourselves of this gracious privilege, and would become the eternal losers.

We are very apt to measure the possibilities of grace by our own experiences and observation, and are inclined to want to limit what God can do for others by what He has done for us. The majority of the human family have always had a tendency to take the path of least resistance; the beaten trail that has been traveled by the majority is more likely to appeal to the average man than that which calls for special effort, pain and sacrifice to travel. If the world had depended upon the average man for the wonderful discoveries of science and the products of invention we would likely have been many centuries behind with our modern blessings and conveniences. Somebody had to venture off the beaten trail of custom and pry into the secrets of the unknown to bring to us the many advantages that we are enjoying today. The biographies of explorers and inventors are wonderfully interesting, and their tasks often extremely difficult, to give to the world the product of their achievements, because of the skeptical attitude of the average person. Alexander Bell was an outstanding example of this fact. After he had constructed the telephone, it was next to impossible to get anyone that had sufficient confidence in his project to finance it for him. Skepticism, however, is not confined to the realm of research and discovery, but is a stumbling block in the way of many in the realm of spiritual things, especially to those who are reluctant to leave the old beaten trail of ritualism and rutualism, for the glorious liberty of the children of God. Because of this fact many are inclined to look with suspicion upon a life of practical holiness, as being far too high a standard to be practiced by man in this life.

The Bible may contain many mysteries, "and some things hard to be understood," but it certainly does not leave the reader in doubt as to the standard of character and life that God purposes shall be the result of his wonderful plan of redemption. Some things are revealed so clearly as to put them beyond the realms of controversy. It seems to the writer it would be a calamity for God to demand a certain standard of Christian integrity to see Him, and then not make sufficiently plain just what that standard was to be. We believe it is sufficiently clear to any unprejudiced mind, and call the reader's attention to the following facts. (1) The Bible reveals the existence of two great personages, namely: God and Satan. In fact, the basis of our knowledge of God and Satan is confined to the pages of inspiration. If it had not been for the Old and New Testaments, we would have known nothing of Jehovah, nor of Satan. (2) The Bible does not

merely reveal the existence of these two great personages, but it goes a step farther and reveals the character of each of them. It makes very plain the fact
that the God of Scripture is a holy God, one who loves
holiness and hates sin; while the Satan of Scripture is
a Satan that is sinful, and one that hates holiness and
loves sin. In fact, they are just the opposite in their
character and desires. What God is, Satan is not, and
what Satan is, God is not. One cannot read his Bible
without conceding this fact. (3) The Scriptures do
not only reveal the existence of these two great personages, and their character, but it goes another step and
reveals the purpose of each of them. Strange to say,
that while they are opposite in their character, they
are identical in their purpose; that is, they are both
seeking to get to themselves a following in the world.
This can only be done by making their followers like
unto themselves in character. God is seeking to make
His people holy, and Satan is seeking to make his followers sinful. In the very nature of the case this is
the only successful way they could hope to have a following of free moral agents, and have them in harmony
with themselves. God could never agree to get along
with sin. He would not have it in heaven; He would
not have it in Eden; and He will not have it in His
people today; for He is the God that changeth not.

Satan could never be content with holy subjects,
for what concord hath light with darkness or "Christ
with Belial?" The fact is, one can very safely determine where one stands in the realms of spiritual things
by his attitude upon this matter of holiness. If the

reader is taking his stand as an advocate of a sinning religion, and making light of and repudiating holiness as a present possibility, through the blood of Christ, such a person is unquestionably in harmony with Satan in regard to this matter, and he and the devil are agreed upon it. If the reader is hungering and thirsting after righteousness, he is manifesting the normal attitude of a Christian. If he is antagonistic to holiness, it is a public advertisement that he is out of fellowship and harmony with God. It is physically and morally impossible for a person to ridicule and speak sarcastically and make light of the very fundamental attribute of God's nature, and at the same time be a loving and devoted disciple of the Almighty. Let the reader not misunderstand us in this matter; we do not unchristianize every person who does not endorse the "second blessing" theory of holiness; it is not the theory for which we contend, in calling the reader's attention to the standard, but the thing itself; not the manner of holiness, but the matter of holiness. No man can object to a holy life and a pure heart and oppose the standard of Christian integrity as being that of holiness, and at the same time be a faithful follower of a God who is holy, who loves holiness and who hates sin. The devil is never any better pleased and can have no more faithful followers than those who profess to be disciples of Christ, and who divide their time in trying to serve God and ridicule holiness. Would the reader know how much God is pleased with you? Measure God's pleasure with you by your pleasure in holiness.

A holy God, a holy heaven, a holy constituency, is the purpose of the Almighty now, and always has been, as is indicated by the fact that He chose us in Jesus Christ before the foundation of the world to be holy, and without blame before him in love (Eph. 1:4). We know there are many orders and ranks in heaven, angels, archangels, cherubims, seraphims, principalities and powers; in just what manner these various creatures may differ, we may not be able to say exactly; but we do know that they all agree in one quality, that is, they are all holy. It is strange, indeed, that men will talk about being happy with Jesus in heaven by and by, when it never seems to have entered into their minds that before they can be happy with Him in heaven, they must first learn the secret of being happy with Him on earth; and that they can never hope to be happy with a holy God without being in harmony with holiness themselves. If people oppose and hate holiness as bitterly when they get to heaven as they do in this world, what a place heaven is destined to be for them. They will enjoy it about as much as they would enjoy a service here for its promotion. A holiness opposing professor of religion would be about as pleased and happy in heaven, as if one who loves the things of the world were forced to attend prayer service, and go to church, when he much preferred to go to the dance.

Holiness is not a sort of appendage to Christianity; it is the very substance, the very kernel, of the thing itself. Does the reader think that Jesus prayed for nothing higher, and died for nothing better, than to make carnal church members? This is a fact, however, unless it is possible to be delivered from all sin. Now if the Bible emphatically declares that, "Without holiness no man shall see the Lord," and sanctification does not make us holy and remove all sin, *we must rewrite the Bible, or preach a better gospel than the Bible advocates, or no one will ever see the Lord.* We must, therefore, either find a work of grace that will make men holy, or they are destined to find themselves forever short of the divine requisite to see the Lord. If the holiness that is revealed in the Bible does not save us from all sin, inward and outward; then we must either rewrite the Bible and incorporate in its teachings a holiness that will do it, or we must get a better gospel somewhere else that will meet the needs; or else man is to find himself in the possession of a malady from which there is no hope of deliverance; and unless there is a post mortem salvation for him that will meet the need, he is forever disqualified for seeing the Lord.

The blood of Jesus Christ is the one healing balm for the festering sore of sin. If there is no hope in the provision made on Calvary, then we are without hope, for there is no name given under heaven whereby men may be saved, except the name of Jesus. It is through His Son Jesus Christ that God purposes to give us the right and fitness for an inheritance incorruptible and undefiled, and that fadeth not away, which He has reserved in heaven for His people. Jesus Christ fits heaven for us, and then fits us for heaven. He goes to prepare mansions for their tenants, and sends the Holy Spirit to prepare the tenants for the mansions by making them pure in heart.

It was the pleasure of the writer to attend the Sunday school in which the late Hon. William Jennings Bryan had his famous class, in Royal Palm Park, Miami, Fla. "In the study of the beatitudes," says Mr. Bryan, "I asked the members of my adult class which they considered of first importance. The sixth received the highest vote." And he adds, "What can be more important than the cleansing of the heart of all that obstructs one's view of God?" The reader may rest assured that whatever else he may or may not possess, when the crisis comes the priceless gem of heart purity will prove to be the divine requisite for fitness for heavenly citizenship and harmonious associations in the abode of God. In fact, "No holiness, no heaven," is as true as the old adage, "No cross, no crown." If the great and good God had made no provision for your entrance to heaven, you would have looked upon Him as a cruel and heartless tyrant, but now that provision is made to give you the fitness of fellowship with God, why should such provision, which is made at infinite cost, be so shamefully neglected? People are not holy because they are in heaven, but they are in heaven because they are holy. Heaven does not make holiness, but holiness makes heaven. It is not the walls of jasper, streets of gold, or gates of pearl that make heaven; these are only incidental; holiness is the basic and fundamental quality of heaven and is the standard without which no man shall see the Lord. It will be as impossible for a man to be

happy in heaven without it as it would be to see
without light or hear in the absence of sound. Holiness, not happiness, is the primary idea of heaven.
Holiness first, happiness second; holiness the cause,
happiness the effect. No amount of sarcasm or ridicule of this truth can change the scriptural statements
regarding it. Holiness is the doctrine of divine revelation, and the Bible and sound reason will remain the
same upon the subject, regardless of the unfounded
and unkind criticisms on the part of its antagonists,
even though some of these be popular and noted divines.

In an outburst of sarcasm on one occasion a person
said, "I think this doctrine of holiness or sanctification, or whatever you call it, is a little far fetched."
Another party nearby spoke up in reply and said,
"Surely it is, it was fetched all the way from heaven."

The purpose of the plan of salvation is to make
men holy, as the apostle well states when he says,
"Now the end of the commandment is charity [love]
out of a *pure heart*, and of a good conscience, and of
faith unfeigned." Can any person by the most far
stretched limit of his imagination suppose that an infinite God with unlimited resources at His command,
who hates sin, and who is holy Himself, would make a
plan of salvation that provided for the continuance of
sin? Would He make a plan of salvation that would
fall short of its objective? Though He infinitely hates
sin, has He provided for man to sin and be saved?
When the last analysis is made, He has either provided
for holiness or He has provided for sin. Think of

God's hating sin, and making provisions for its continuance.

If a doctor had a son grievously afflicted, would he not use all his knowledge of medicine and surgery, and do the best he was capable of doing to heal him? If a lawyer had a son whose properties were involved in litigation, would he not use all his ability relative to the legal technicalities involved in his son's interests in order to do his very best for him? Can the reader conceive of an infinite God, with wisdom and power at His command, doing any less for His creatures? Would He do less than His best, or at least less than the need would require. Does not the apostle say, "My God shall supply all your need"? What greater need has the human family than to be delivered from the curse of sin? Has He not promised to deliver us out of the hands of our enemies? What greater enemy has mankind than sin? Do these promises mean that He will supply all our needs, except the greatest need we have, the need to be made holy; do they mean that he will deliver us from all our enemies, except our greatest enemy, which is sin? The greatest need that any human being can have is the need to be delivered from the curse of sin.

Let the reader glance at the following Scriptures: Heb. 13:12; Titus 2:14; Eph. 4:1; 2 Thess. 2:13; 1 Peter 1:5; 1 Peter 1:22; 1 Peter 2:21, 22; Heb. 12:10. These and others of like quality show conclusively that the standard of New Testament Christianity is that of heart purity. Can the reader believe that God would make statements of this character, and then never permit us to be the partakers of their benefits. This would cast reflection upon His veracity and power, and represent Him as making a plan of salvation, of which no one was to be the recipient. It represents him as making a plan of salvation that falls short of its objective; and as being Himself, without the inclination or power (or both) to carry into execution a plan that He, himself, designed. It represents Him as being a tyrannical master who is demanding impossibilities of his subjects, because he has made no adequate provision to morally or physically measure up to the demands he has thrust upon them. This is not the God of the New Testament who said, "How much more shall your Father which is in heaven give good things to them that ask him?" Of what value is the plan of salvation to us, if no one is ever to realize its benefits? The last word upon the subject is simply this, either God's provisions are worthless and mere mockery, or else He can make us pure and holy in this life; in which case holiness is the New Testament standard of moral and spiritual possibility for the disciples of Jesus Christ.

Says the Rev. John A. Wood, "The minimum of salvation is salvation from sinning, the maximum is salvation from pollution." This, of course, includes outward and inward sin, *all sin*.

Systems of truth, and all enterprises which are the product of intelligence, have a definite objective or chief purpose to which all the qualities of such truth must work. Many illustrations of this fact could be found: schools for culture, governments for protection, machinery for quick and labor saving production, hospitals for physical healing, automobiles for locomotion. The automobile has its many mechanical parts, different in their construction and design and manner of operation, but the aggregate purpose of all combined is a means of conveyance. The plan of salvation which God has instituted for fallen man, is to restore unto him his lost inheritance, to make him holy; and while there may be many intricate parts of this great plan, the aggregate aim of all of them combined is to make men holy. Look at Gethsemane, Calvary, and all the tragic scenes in the ministry of our Lord; remember how His life was freighted with blessing to mankind everywhere; it may all be summed up in one sentence, "He went about doing good;" but what was the ultimate objective? It was to make men holy, pure in heart, so as to conform with New Testament demands, New Testament doctrine, and the standards of New Testament Christianity.

CHAPTER V

A Bit of Misinformation

Misinformation and prejudice are always detrimental to the solution of any problem. Perhaps there is no problem within the realm of Bible truth to which there is so much criticism offered, upon the basis of misinformation and prejudice, as to the doctrine and experience of sanctification. Most of the objection and antagonism to this matter is based upon those things that are usually no part of the experience or doctrine. Probably from seventy to eighty per cent of the opposition is the product of misinformation.

It is never safe to get our convictions concerning religious truth out of the lives of those that profess it. Let the Word of God be the basis of your doctrine. There have always been men who were extremists, fanatics, enthusiasts; men who were hysterical and excessive in their emotions. Mr. Wesley had his Maxwell and Bell, and the modern holiness people are not without their problems along this line.

It often happens that there are people who are very unfair in their criticisms of religious truth, and usually measure the quality of the truth by the poorest example of it to be found in the community. They usually pick some person who is mentally deficient or hypocritically crooked, and with great bluster and blow proceed to inform the community that they are as good as such individuals who profess so much. They do not seem to be aware of the terrible slander they give themselves in making comparison of themselves with the weak-minded and hypocritical. No doubt there are some who have always been shallow, narrow minded, ignorant and impulsive, whose nonsense has brought sacred things into disrepute and reproach; but you and I, dear reader, cannot afford to ignore what God has written for our edification because someone else has made a dunce of himself.

Let us look into some of the grounds, or seeming grounds rather, which form the basis of misinformation and prejudice. First of all and possibly foremost, is that time worn objection that nobody can live without sin in this world. We have covered this objection to some extent in the chapter entitled, "A Human Being," and will therefore only touch the matter briefly. First, let us say, that no reputable teacher of holiness teaches that it is impossible for a sanctified man to sin. God never takes away by grace that which He gave us by nature. As man came from the hand of his Creator, he was a free moral agent, he is so today and always will be. It is upon this fact that the entire plan of redemption is based. The will is the determining factor in our conduct, and neither sin nor grace destroys it. I can be a sinner *if I will;* I can be a Christian *if I will.* If the writer knew of a work of grace that would destroy the possibility or power to sin, instead of being afraid of it, we would become an urgent seeker for its benefits. Unfortunately there is no such grace. However, any man that has brought his will into subjection to the will of God does not sin (1 John 3:9). The normal Christian life in regeneration is a life that is victorious over sin. Your objection is based upon the wrong grounds in this matter; therefore you should be objecting to regeneration, and not sanctification, if your objection is the matter of living victorious over sin. If the reader is professing to be a Christian, and doing those things that he would not do if he were sanctified, the probability is the reader is not converted. Yea, let all the "sin or bust" theologians, and all the "When I would do good evil is present with me" crowd, and all the "none righteous, no, not one" church members, *know all men by these presents,* they are as yet unconverted, and are Christian in nothing but name, and that is a sad contradiction. The mark of discrimination between a Christian and a sinner is found in 1 John 3:8, 10. Let the reader examine himself accordingly. In a word, sanctification does not destroy our free moral agency. A sanctified man can sin, he may sin, but no Christian *must sin.*

But says the objector, "Does not sanctification make it impossible for one to have his feelings wounded?" The fact that you have been the recipient of any degree of grace, large or small, does not make you less human. This in itself ought to answer the question. God is grieved; Jesus was grieved; the Holy Spirit was grieved; we certainly cannot anticipate any work of grace exalting us above the Trinity. There are many things that may wound the feelings of a sanctified person. It is said that Jesus died of a

broken heart, sorrow and grief over a lost world broke
His heart and He died prematurely, and not according
to nature or custom, as was shown by the fact that
though it was often necessary to break the bones of
the suffering victims of crucifixion, when they came to
Jesus for that purpose they found Him already dead.
It might well have been written upon His tomb, "He
died of a broken heart." Sanctification will not make
it impossible for you to feel, either mentally or physically, and you may find yourself in heaviness for various reasons, in sorrow and in affliction. Sanctification
is not a warranty deed to nothing but happiness all the
remainder of one's life. It guarantees nothing except
the deliverance from sin.

Sanctification is sometimes misrepresented, as being an experience of unbroken joy or exuberance, a
place where human discouragement, or social sorrow,
or days of sadness are driven away forever by the tri-
umphant entrance of unbroken bliss and happiness.
This might possibly be the experience of the exception
to the rule; but we are frank to say the holiest of saints
are not without their perplexing problems, and often
find themselves in the midst of heaviness, sometimes
through manifold temptations, or perhaps loss of
friends, or financial adversity, maybe physical affliction, in fact, a multitude of intricate problems have a
tendency to put upon the disciple of Jesus Christ, regardless of the degree of grace he may possess, a spirit
of depression, a sense of loneliness, or a feeling of sadness. Elijah may seek the shelter of the juniper tree;
Jacob may say, "Ye have bereaved me of my children;

Joseph is not, Simeon is not, and ye will take away Benjamin; all these things are against me;" while the dear old patriarch Job may say with pathetic voice, "The Lord giveth and the Lord taketh away, blessed be the name of the Lord;" and while these words may have a note of victory in them, they also sound a note of sorrow; of one who has suffered much loss. Even the blessed Christ is heard saying, "My soul is exceeding sorrowful even unto death." These and many like expressions show conclusively that holy character is not always unmixed with sorrow and sadness.

Discouragements may come, even to the sanctified soul, through persecution, through false accusations, by being ostracized and criticized; these and many other problems make the sanctified life to be freighted with responsibilities, and many times necessitate its undergoing hardships. Sanctification is something more than a mere whoop and hurrah, it is a life of obligation and service, a life of devotion and fidelity to a cause that is unpopular, in a world that has ever been unfriendly to grace.

Says the Rev. John A. Wood, in answering the question, "Will sanctification enable me to pray, believe, and rejoice every moment even in the severest of trials?" "It will, doubtless, so far as it is naturally, or perhaps I should say physically possible. While the soul may have seasons of heaviness, sore conflicts, and protracted trials, which are often very necessary; it may still possess a heaven of peace and love and light in its ocean depths. This enables the sanctified soul to pray, believe, and rejoice every moment, or to 'rejoice evermore, pray without ceasing, and in everything give thanks."

Mr. Wesley said, "Nay, the mind itself may be deeply distressed, exceedingly sorrowful, may be perplexed and pressed down with heaviness and anguish, even unto agony; while the heart cleaves to God by perfect love, and the will is wholly resigned to Him." Certainly a man may always rejoice in the consciousness of God's presence, and in the fact of His divine favor, so that in the midst of sorrow and afflictions, and misunderstandings, there is an abiding, self-satisfying evidence of the approbation of heaven's King; thus enabling us to say with the apostle, "sorrowful yet always rejoicing."

What about anger? Is it compatible with sanctification? Do the people known as holiness, or sanctified people, not teach that it is impossible for them to get angry? No reputable teacher of the doctrine of sanctification advocates the impossibility of becoming angry, for the same reason that no reputable teacher would teach the impossibility of sin. But you ask, "Is anger compatible with holy character?" There certainly can be no doubt but what there is some kind of anger that is accordant with holy character; such Scriptures as, "Who can abide in the fierceness of his anger?" (Nah. 1:6), "For mine anger is turned away from him" (Hosea 14:4), "God is angry with the wicked every day" (Psalm 7:11), "And when he had looked round about on them with anger" (Mark 3:5), and many others, indicate beyond a doubt that there is a quality of anger that is possible, even in the experience of holiness; otherwise God could not be angry, and Jesus would not have been angered.

The truth about this matter is to be found in a proper discrimination, between a holy or righteous anger, and a carnal anger. We know that in spite of a clear exegesis of this matter some will be inclined to excuse themselves in the manifestation of carnal anger, under the guise that they were righteously indignant. No interpretation of the Word of God could be made that is not susceptible of abuse, and we are not responsible for those who are dishonest in their statements relative to personal experience. Most people can detect the difference between a carnal manifestation of anger, and a manifestation of anger that is righteous, if they will lay aside any tendency they may have to shield themselves. But if there is a distinction to be made, how can we know and be able to discriminate between carnal and righteous anger?

Carnal anger is that anger which is selfish and revengeful in its nature, is purely carnal and seeks personal gratification in seeing the object of its wrath made to suffer; it takes delight in wreaking its vengeance upon the cause of its manifestation; in a word, it takes pleasure in getting even with that particular person or persons which causes its temperamental disturbance.

Holy anger is an anger that never has any selfish or revengeful attitude toward anyone. It is not an anger that is the product of any selfish desire to avenge ourselves, *but is a righteous resentment of that which is wrong, and has as its motive only the best good of the object of its rebuke, and a desire to honor and glorify God and exalt righteousness.* The anger of God and our Savior was not wrong and was nothing more nor less than a holy indignation and righteous resentment of that which was wrong. The absence of such an anger as this is a sinful defect in many who profess high standards of grace. Would you not think there was a moral or spiritual deficiency in a man that could stand by and hear God's name blasphemed, His cause misrepresented, His people ridiculed and souls misled, and never feel any stirrings within? It is the lack of this very thing in some of the modern preachers (that is the inclination to be stirred or become righteously indignant), that is the cause of so much wickedness being practiced by professors of Christianity. They are allowed to live in all kinds of sin, and sit under the preacher's ministry Sunday after Sunday without a single rebuke because a velvelt-mouthed, easy-going, "all things to all men" kind of a minister is never stirred at the hypocrisy and inconsistency of his congregation. Would to God we might have a clergy who would be stirred, as Paul's heart was stirred within him when he preached at Athens, as he looked upon the wickedness and idolatry there. Give us a people and a ministry whose holy indignation and righteous anger will be stirred until there will be some rebuking of sin, now and then at least, somewhere besides in the pulpit. Pure or holy anger is never followed by condemnation nor regret; on the contrary there is an inward satisfaction of having performed one's righteous duty. Carnal anger is always followed by condemnation and guilt the same as any other sin. A sanctified man may manifest a holy anger, that is, a righteous resentment toward that which is wrong, but no sanctified man can be carnally angry and keep in divine favor.

The reader may ask how he is to discriminate between carnal and righteous anger. We have tried to make a clear and scriptural distinction; yet it is probable that an inward sense of condemnation if honestly adhered to, would go a long way to determine the matter for us. Anything that produces condemnation, we may well rest assured, is not for our good and is displeasing to God. An honest course of procedure at this delicate point may go a long way to help settle a very intricate and difficult problem. Let us be angry at nothing but sin, and be sure that such anger is nothing more than the product of an earnest desire to benefit the offender and glorify God. Such anger may prove a virtue rather than a sin. Only an anger that seeks the best good of the subject at which it is directed, and at the same time can love such subject, and purposes only to glorify God and rebuke sin, is in accord with a wholly sanctified man.

CHAPTER VI

WHAT IS IT?

The words sanctify, sanctifieth, and sanctification are used in the Old and New Testaments about one hundred and forty-one times. It would be folly to ignore a matter that has been mentioned in both parts of the Scripture so often as this. Certainly a subject of such importance is worthy of our unprejudiced and serious consideration. A right understanding of the definition of terms and phraseology is the basis of all true interpretation. It will be impossible to agree as to doctrines as long as our interpretation, or defining rather, of words are at variance. Anyone who reads the numerous Scriptures containing the word sanctification and its synonyms, cannot fail to know there is something in the realms of religious experience that is therein signified. It would seem that whatever it is, and whatever relation it sustains to Christian experience, that it is the will of God (1 Thes. 4:3), that it is within the realm of possibility (Heb. 2:11), that God has provided it for us at the infinite sacrifice of His own Son (Heb. 13:12, 13, 1 Cor. 1:31), and that it occupies a very large place in the prayers and exhortations of Jesus and His apostles (1 Thes. 5:23, Heb. 6:1, 1 Thes. 4:7, 8). Whatever significance these Scriptures had relative to Christian experience at the time of their inspiration and utterance, the reader may well rest assured they sustain the same today.

There is some truth in the world that is contingent, and some that is eternal. By contingent truth we mean that truth that is sustained by certain prevailing conditions and dependent upon them. By eternal truth we mean that which is based upon the inexorable law of nature or science. Contingent truth which is dependent upon conditions is fluctuating, that is, what may be true today may be false tomorrow, as for example: I might say that it is raining today; the truth of that statement is contingent, for it is dependable upon the weather, and while it may be true today, the same statement tomorrow may be false; but if I say that two and two are four, it will be true today, tomorrow and for all time for it is based upon an unchanging law of mathematical science. Two and two are four now and will be forever, here and everywhere else in the world, because it is not dependent upon changing circumstances. It may be that what is wrong in one state today, may be right tomorrow, (that is legally speaking) for the right or wrong of the matter is dependent upon the statute of that particular commonwealth at the time of its execution; but that which is morally wrong in one place and time is morally wrong any place, all the time. The Word of God is immutable and whatever these scriptures meant at the time of their inspiration and utterance, they mean today; for the truth of sanctification is not based upon environments nor surrounding circumstances but upon the unchanging word of Jehovah.

If the basis of interpretation is a clear defining and understanding of terms, let us observe a few definitions of the word sanctification and its relative terms. Whatever these words mean in every day language we must remember they mean the same in Scripture. We must never think that because words are found in the Bible, that they have a peculiar significance or a kind of superhuman, weird, or ghostly meaning. It is likewise a serious mistake to try to confine the word to one definition when it is plainly evident that it is not confined to one meaning. Sanctification, like many other words in the English language, is not confined to one meaning, and to so apply it to Biblical interpretation, is to find ourselves in a maze of confusion and contradictions. It means "to set apart," "to consecrate," "to make holy," to reverence or make sacred"; but we submit to the reader also the theological definition as given in Webster's International Dictionary: "The act or process of God's grace, by which the affections of men are purified or alienated from sin and the world, and exalted to a supreme love of God; also state of thus being purified." Sanctify from Latin, *sanctificare; sanctus*—holy, and *ficare*—to make;" thus the literal meaning is, to make holy. "To make free from sin; to cleanse from moral corruption and pollution; to purify." Webster then gives Jno. 17:17 as an example of its use; thus confirming the teaching of the Protestant church.

We further submit to the reader the definition of consecration, which is often interpreted by some as being identical with sanctification. Consecrate is defined, "to set apart, to dedicate, to appropriate to sacred uses." Consecration is defined, "The act or ceremony of consecrating; state of being consecrated." The reader will note that while sanctification embraces the matter of consecration; consecration does not include sanctification in the theological sense of purification, and the word consecrate or consecration is never defined so as to include the cleansing or purifying of the soul. Consecration is rather the condition upon which sanctification is obtained; just as repentance is the condition upon which justification is obtained. We must not overlook the fact that consecration is an act of volitional quality, and comes entirely within the limits of man's free moral agency; consecration is the act of man in his own behalf, while sanctification is an act of God's grace by which men's hearts are purified and made holy.

In his book entitled, "Sanctification, the Experience and the Ethics," Rev. Roy T. Williams, D. D., very forcibly and convincingly says, "If consecration is sanctification, or if sanctification is consecration, and that only; then it is all purely human, and God has little or nothing to do with it, except to accept the work done by man. This position could never be justified or defended." The apostle Paul says, "For both he that sanctifieth and they who are sanctified, are all of one: for which cause he is not ashamed to call them brethren." It cannot be that He that sanctifieth and they who are sanctified are one and the same in this text. Two distinct and definite persons are herewith brought to the reader's attention; the one

that does the sanctifying, and the one that is sanctified. If God alone, is referred to in this Scripture,
then we have the absurdity of God consecrating men;
if man alone is both the sanctifier and the sanctified,
the whole matter is entirely human. This is both unreasonable and unscriptural (Heb. 13:12, 13).

But the question may be asked, If sanctification
has so many meanings in the Word of God, when we
read our Bibles, how can we tell what definition to
confer upon it? The answer to this need not be at all
difficult. Frankly speaking, we would say, the best
way to ascertain its meaning is to use the same degree
of common sense that you use when you read any other
book or paper. If you were reading the evening news,
and you came to a word that had a variety of meanings, how would you determine the definition of that
word? Do you not give such meaning to the word as
is plainly indicated by the manner in which it is used,
and the relation it bears to the subject? Thus all the
reader need do, to understand how to define a term, is
to take into consideration the manner in which it is
used. Let us give here a single example by way of
illustration. Take the word "forge," here is a word
with a variety of meanings. It means "to hammer out
or shape a piece of metal," "it is an open fireplace
with forced draft for heating metal," "To make a
false imitation of that which is genuine," "To go slow-
ly with difficulty." Now let us use the word in a sentence and see if we have any difficulty in ascertaining
its meaning. "Mr. A— forged Mr. B—'s signature at
the First National Bank today." Now would the

reader have any difficulty in determining the meaning
of the word "forge" in this sentence? Certainly not.
We can tell by the manner in which it is used. Now
let us take the word in question, (sanctify) and use
the same rule relative to a passage of scripture. If
the term sanctify is used relative to something that
man is to do or ought to do, and has relation to a volitional act on his part you may know it is not an act of
divine grace; but if it has relation to something that
God is to do, then it must be an operation of His grace
that is beyond the power of man to accomplish. Take
for illustration the prayer of Jesus. What does sanctification mean in this prayer? "Sanctify them." Is
He talking about separation; is it consecration; is it to
reverence; or is it to make holy? That it does not
mean separation is seen by the fact that they have already reached that place where it can be said of them
that, "They are not of the world, even as I am not of
the world"; that it did not mean to reverence God,
or consecrate themselves may be seen from the fact
that both of these things come within the realm of
man's volitional action and free moral agency, while
the kind of sanctification that He is speaking of in this
text, is the kind the Father is to do. Man makes his
own consecration, consequently the kind of sanctification that is the matter of discussion here is not consecration, for this sanctification is to be executed as a
divine act. "Father, ... sanctify them." It is
therefore an act of God's grace, as defined by Webster,
and confirmed by the Holy Scriptures. This gives it
both etymological and scriptural soundness. Sanctifi-

cation in its most common sense in the New Testament, therefore, is an act of God's grace; an operation of the Holy Spirit by which the subject is cleansed and made holy; so that one may be able to comply with the scriptural command, "As he which hath called you is holy, *so be ye holy* in all manner of living" (R. V.), thus enabling one to follow peace with all men and possess that holiness, "without which no man shall see the Lord." In defining sanctification we would say that while incidentally, it does sometimes mean to set apart, to consecrate, to reverence, and to make sacred, yet the fundamental and generally accepted use of the word in New Testament writing is to make pure, or holy, as theologically defined by Webster, and scripturally confirmed by the "Thus saith the Lord." This is theologically, etymologically and scripturally true.

Let the reader remember that sanctification does not mean anything more or less than the being fully consecrated to God, baptized with the Holy Spirit and cleansed from all sin, and made a partaker of that holiness, without which no man shall see the Lord. There is nothing extreme, fanatical, or ridiculous about this, and nothing more than what every Christian ought to earnestly desire and seek. "Blessed are they that hunger and thirst after righteousness."

Before leaving the matter of defining sanctification, we will call the reader's attention to the relation that it sustains to other salvation terms. The three outstanding terms employed in the plan of redemption are: justification, regeneration and sanctification.

Take the term "justify" first, (we are defining these words according to Webster's International Dictionary) the theological definition "To accept and receive those as just or righteous who believe in Christ, or to make them righteous by infusing grace into them." The next term is "regenerate" "To cause to be spiritually born again." And last the word "sanctify," "To cleanse from moral corruption." It certainly must be plain to the reader that these three terms have a different meaning, and sustain a different relation to Christian experience. It is true that justification and regeneration are concomitant and coexist. The reader may ask, "If these can take place simultaneously, why may we not include sanctification, and thus at a single stroke restore man to his divine image?" We offer as an answer to this question, that justification is not a moral change in man's nature, and is not in itself, properly speaking, a work of grace; but is rather a relative change which accompanies regeneration, that changes the relation between God and his hitherto sinning subject. There are but two great master strokes in the building of Christian character; regeneration, the impartation of spiritual life; sanctification, the cleansing of the soul from moral pollution, the inherent or inborn sin.

It would either be the grossest prejudice, or downright ignorance on the part of any person, it seems, to try to make these terms mean the same thing, and to sustain the same relation to Christian experience. To assume that they are received simultaneously in nowise changes the matter of sanctification, but only has reference to the manner of its obtainment. This we will discuss elsewhere in the following pages. We trust we have given the reader some light in the matter of an etymological, theoretical and Scriptural understanding of the term sanctification and the relation that it sustains to our personal religious experience.

CHAPTER VII

Suppression or Eradication

In the preceding chapter we have tried to clearly define sanctification. To the mind of the writer the relation that sanctification sustains to Christian character and experience, is primarily that of heart purity. Based upon the definitions of the word itself, and upon the teaching of the church in general, and upon the New Testament standard of moral integrity, it is quite clear that holiness, heart purity and sanctification are synonymous terms in their application to Christian character.

The terms wholly sanctified, saved to the uttermost, and cleansed from all sin, must include sin in every form in which it exists. It is a contradiction to say that any person is cleansed from all sin, or saved to the uttermost, when there is sin of any kind still remaining in him. The best that truth could assume in such a case would be that he is only partially cleansed from sin, and partly saved. It would be foolish to say that a man was saved from the drink habit, because he only got drunk at three or six month intervals; it would be ridiculous to say that a man was entirely saved from the affliction of epilepsy because his attacks had been in a measure reduced. Yet it would be no more of an untruth to say a man was saved from his drunkenness completely when he continued to be intoxicated at certain intervals, or that a man was saved from epilepsy entirely, when he continued to have spasms periodically, than it would to say that a man was saved from, or cleansed from, all sin, while he was yet a sinner by practice or sinful by nature. We have not so learned the English language as to interpret, "being cleansed from all sin," and being "holy *as he which hath called you is holy*," to mean that we are still sinners, either by practice or by nature. To be saved to the uttermost, to be cleansed from all sin, to be wholly sanctified, most assuredly implies the being delivered from sin in all its forms, or the English language can no longer be depended upon to convey ideas. Do such scriptures as "put off the old man," "crucify the old man," "the blood of Jesus Christ, his son, cleanseth us from all sin," and many like passages only mean that the best God can do for us, is to allow us to struggle along with no promise of deliverance in this world? What about His promise that we should serve Him "without fear, *in holiness and righteousness* before him, all the days of our life"?

In regard to this matter, Dr. R. T. Williams, D. D., in his most excellent book, "Sanctification, the Experience and Ethics," well says, "Here is the great battle ground concerning holiness. The question is simply this: 'Is sin destroyed in the act of sanctification or not?' This is the question on which turns all belief in sanctification. It is folly to try to pass as a believer in holiness and at the same time question its doctrine of eradication. There can be no such thing as holiness in its final analysis without the eradication of sin. Holiness and suppression are incompatible terms. The old man and counteraction make a pale and sickly kind of holiness. It is holiness and eradication or holiness not at all. . . . If one does not believe in eradication of sin in the heart he does not believe in holiness. His belief in eradication is the determining factor in his attitude toward the great doctrine of full salvation. This is the crux of the whole matter, and it is useless to juggle words or become confused in hair splitting theological discussions concerning holiness. There is one question to settle, can God destroy sin utterly, and does He do it in this life?" These words of Dr. Williams are quite to the point and place the matter beyond the realm of controversy or debate.

Let the reader not overlook the fact that the scriptural injunction is, "But *as he* which hath called you is holy, so be ye holy." What kind of holiness are we to have? The kind God has. *As He* which hath called you is holy, *so be ye*. Is God's holiness a holiness that is mixed with sin? Is God's holiness one that is busy suppressing a sinful nature that is in antagonism to it? If so, then suppression is the kind you are to have; and like as suppression is God's great problem relative to sin; so your continual problem is to be the same, for your holiness is to be like God's. But if God's holiness is unmixed, if yours is to be like His, yours must likewise be unmixed, if you are to measure up to the scriptural standard of, *"As he* which hath called you is holy, *so be ye."* If the statement of 1 Pet. 1:15 does not teach that we are to have the same kind of holiness that God has, then the scripture is very misleading. If this language does not teach the complete separation from sin, we doubt if there are any words in the English language that could convey such meaning. This language could not teach suppression without implying that God was sinful; for if we have holiness like as He which hath called us; and our holiness is mixed with sin; then God's holiness must necessarily be the same. If God's holiness is pure, then ours to be like His, must also be pure. To say this is not to imply that we are equal with God, but merely that we are to be the partakers of His holiness and we are to have an imparted and not an imputed holiness (Heb. 12:10; 2 Pet. 1:14). If I go down to the Mississippi River and dip up a cupful of water, this in nowise implies that I have the Mississippi River in my cup; but I have some of the same kind of water that is in the river. When we speak of being holy as He which hath called us is holy, we do not put ourselves upon an equality with God, in the possession of infallible or absolute holiness; but we do declare that we have been the partakers of the divine nature, and cleansed from all sin, that is, made partakers of *His holiness*.

If the Holy Spirit knew the meaning of such phraseology as, "as he" "is holy" "so be ye," "cleanseth from all sin," and other expressions; then the least we can say, is that He meant for us to be, whatever these terms indicate in their generally accepted meaning. By what manner of interpretation can pure be made to mean suppression? Peter left no doubt as to whether the baptism with the Holy Ghost was suppression or eradication; when relating what occurred on the day of Pentcost, he said, "Their hearts *had been* purified by faith" (Acts 15:8, 9). We would like to ask some of the advocates of the doctrine of suppression or counteraction if this language teaches suppression. If so, would they please submit some language which would convey the idea of eradication? In a word, what would or could be said to teach eradication any more clearly?

A typical example of the suppressionist doctrine may be seen in the following extract taken from a letter from one of them, to a friend of the writer. The occasion of this letter was some criticism that was being made of a book which was teaching the eradication of sin. He says, "Now don't misunderstand my position, nor draw the conclusion from what I have said, that I advocate suppression, or counteraction, I do not. These theories are just as unscriptural as eradication." Let us pause just here in the quotation long enough to say, that while we notice the brother denies being a suppressionist, or a counteractionist, or an eradicationist, and denounces them all as being unscriptural, he fails to tell us just what he is. He declares that all of these positions are wrong, but offers us no solution to the problem. For a long time we were in a quandary to know just what to call the dear brother, until one day in reading a few lines farther in his letter we detected his position, when he said, "I believe, have proved, teach and experience daily the blessed deliverance which comes to spirit, soul and body, through reckoning yourself dead indeed unto sin, and alive unto God, through the faith of the Son of God. Thus I am forgiven of all my sins, justified freely of all things, regenerated, renewed to the image of God, sanctified *in* Christ Jesus, baptized in the Holy Ghost, *my heart is cleansed from all sin*." After reading these lines I learned that he was what I am pleased to call an imputationist. That is, as you note he is sanctified *in* Christ. That is to say that through the holiness of Christ he is accounted holy, because Christ was holy. This is rather an imputed sanctification, than an actual experience of holiness. That is to say that while he is yet carnal, because Christ was holy, and he believes in Christ as the Savior, he is accounted as holy, though in fact he is not. He is merely accounted holy because of Christ's righteousness, his holiness is imputed rather than possessed. In other words, reducing this to the maximum of simplicity, it is simply this: Because Christ was holy, and he believes in the name of Christ, therefore Christ accepts him as holy, though in fact he is not holy at all. This is what is implied by being sanctified *in* Christ. That is to say, while I am not holy, God looks not at me, but at Jesus, and *accounts* me as being holy for Jesus' sake; though in fact I do not believe in eradication, and acknowledge I do not possess any such experience. This is too much like the old negro, who, when weeping over her departed husband, she said, "Oh Sambo! Sambo! I do hopes youse gone whar I specks you ain't."

Jesus said, "Blessed are the pure in heart." But

there are no pure in heart unless eradication is possible; for a heart with sin in it is not pure. In the preceding letter of this good brother he reaches the climax of absurdity when he says he does not believe in eradication and then gives testimony that the blood of Jesus cleanses him from all sin. Surely, Jesus would not bless a class of people that did not exist and never could exist, yet he says, "Blessed are the pure in heart." How can suppression or any other plan than eradication produce a standard such as is revealed in Matt. 5:8, or 1 Pet. 1:22 and similar passages?

It is the object of Jesus to save us from all iniquity and *purify* unto Himself a peculiar people (Tit. 2:14). This is not a relative purity consisting of Christ's righteousness being imputed unto us; but is a personal, inwrought cleansing. That it is such may be seen from the language of the apostle when he states the purpose of such cleansing, "That he might present it [the church] to himself a glorious church, not having spot or wrinkle, or any such thing; but that it *should be holy* and without blemish." Cleansing from sin, is not an imputation of righteousness, it is not a mere calling that just which is unjust, but it is a making clean from that which is foul, loathesome, or in anyway sinful.

When the prophet was announcing the coming of the Messiah and the nature of His ministry he said, "But who may abide the day of his coming; and who shall stand when he appeareth? For he is like a refiner's fire, and like fuller's sope: and he shall sit as a refiner and purifier of silver, and *he shall purify the sons of Levi,* and *purge them as gold and silver,* that they may offer unto the Lord an offering in righteousness." The language used here cannot be misconstrued, and shows conclusively that the work wrought upon the subject, is that of purification from every objectionable, defective, or sinful thing; thus fitting them for God's service. The very terms used here, "refiner and purifier," suggest the nature of the work that is to be accomplished. He cannot be a purifier unless He purifies; any more than He could be a Savior unless He saved. Both of the material elements used here to denote the nature of the work of the Spirit are instruments of cleansing and purifying. These words, by no means of grammatical jugglery can be made to indicate suppression, counteraction nor imputation. He shall purify and purge, does not mean, we shall suppress. If these words do not indicate a deliverance from the accursed thing we call sin, then there is apparently no dependence to be put in the meaning of words. Not to save us from carnality, is either a reflection on the willingness or the ability of God. A purging from sin that will make the subject clean clear through, and clear through clean, is evidently the purpose of the Almighty, in behalf of all who will submit themselves to Him.

As one writer says, "Jesus himself, is the watchful refiner and like the practiced refiner, He notes the purifying process until the heart becomes so pure that it reflects the divine image; which is nothing less than the brightness of the Father's glory and the express image of His person." Could such a process be compatible with a sinful heart? In showing the need of holiness and also the nature of sin, the Rev. Asbury Lowery says, "Sin is an alien element, alike antagonistic to God, and the interests of men. It is not original in being a part of the primordial make-up of man. It is subsequent inoculation, a seed of evil projected into human nature at a later date. Sin is deadly, therefore it must be destroyed. Any remedy that does not take primal account of sin and aim at its absolute abolition, is insufficient, if not spurious. The gist of sanctification is deliverance from sin."

When David prayed so earnestly, "Wash me throughly from mine iniquity, and cleanse me from my sin" (Psa. 51:2), he was not espousing the doctrine of suppression, nor asking for a mixed holiness discolored with sin; his was a heart cry for deliverance." "Wash me throughly," "purge me." What more could be desired, what less could be expected of a God who hates sin and loves holiness? Thank God! Holiness electrocutes the old man, and electrifies the new man. How can any man analyze such scriptures as Tit. 2:14, 1 Pet. 1:15, Matt. 5:8, 1 Thes. 4:7, and others of like nature, and not find in them personal purity? It might be done only upon the basis of teaching an imputed sanctification, that of being sanctified *in* Christ rather than being sanctified *by* Christ. Such teaching, however, leaves man after all God can do for him, sinful by nature and in all probability a sinner by practice.

Heart purity. I know of nothing more desirable. The wonder is that all are not striving to obtain it. John A. Wood, in his "Perfect Love" says, "Holiness is the same kind in man that it is in God; and certainly there is nothing morally wrong repressed in God. Holiness is unmingled purity; entire sanctification is the cleansing of the soul from all those things repressed in the partially purified heart, so that there is nothing wrong to be repressed." Choking down and repressing sin is not the process of cleansing the heart. Repressive power is nowhere attributed to the blood of Christ; but purgative and cleansing efficacy. Sanctification is the carnal nature eradicated, exterminated, not suppressed. The trouble with most suppressionists is, they nearly paralyze the "old man" on Sunday; but Monday they drag him out, rub him down, give him a little camphor, and the smelling salts, plaster up his shins, give him a good tonic: until by Wednesday night he is so alive and well, that he objects to going to prayermeeting.

We once heard of a man that was upon the point of forsaking the doctrine of eradication, "Because," said he, "there is no use to preach it when I do not see anyone living it. When I do not see it manifest in the lives of professors, I am discouraged in preaching it." We would reply to such statement by saying, "The place to get our religious doctrines, is not in the lives of Christian professors, but from the pages of Holy Writ." The writer is willing to concede that many who profess this great grace, are sadly lacking in the gracious principles, that ought to be manifest in a heart thus purified. But we ask, "Shall we hold the standard where it belongs and try to bring the people up to the Bible standard, or shall we drag the standard down to where the people generally live?"

In further quoting J. A. Wood we agree, "No man is saved by the credit of Christ's holiness without personal holiness begotten in him by Christ; and Christ never accounts His people holy in law, before He makes them holy in fact; our holiness is no more confined to the person of Christ, than a sick man's health is to the physician who attends him. . . . . Through the blood, merit and work of Christ the fully saved soul has personal sanctification and is made holy (not accounted holy because of the holiness of someone else).

Says Dr. Daniel Steele, "God announces himself as holy and binds human obligation to holiness upon this revealed attribute, 'Be ye holy, for I am holy.' Who dares to say that God's holiness is different in kind from man's holiness, save that one is absolute and original and the other is inwrought by the Holy Spirit."

It may be true that we are sanctified in Christ provisionally speaking; for He suffered without the gate to sanctify the people with His own blood. Here is provision for every man, yet while we have sanctification in Christ provisionally, we can only have it experimentally by a mighty operation of the Spirit cleansing and purifying our souls, by obeying the truth. The doctrine of being sanctified in Christ is the ground work for much modern hypocrisy on the part of professing Christians. It is the plan by which we excuse all our inconsistencies, sure enough, we are not right, but Christ was right and because He was right, we do not have to be entirely right; His holiness will make up for any lack of efficiency on our part. We do not claim to be holy, we do not need to, for Christ was holy. "He who brings down Christ's religion to such a low level," says Mark Guy Pierce, "has never learned the meaning of the cross."

No wonder Dr. A. M. Hills asks the question, "Now is it thinkable that Jesus prayed for nothing higher, and died for nothing better, than to leave members of his Church a mass of carnality and inward corruption?" When the infinite God undertakes to sanctify you, make you pure, through and through, in spirit, soul and body, does He still leave every corner of your being infested with a carnality that is at war with God?" Surely by this time the reader must be able to see the inconsistency of professing to have a pure heart, that has never had and never will have sin removed from it in this world.

When we read the beatitudes, "Blessed are they that mourn," does the reader deny such a class? "Blessed are the meek," are there no meek? Blessed are they that hunger and thirst after righteousness," are there none that hunger after righteousness? "Blessed are the merciful," are there no merciful? We believe that these preceding classes all exist. But when it comes to, "Blessed are the pure in heart," many put a question mark behind the possibility of such a class in this world. "Oh," says the objecter, "we believe in a pure heart, but we do not believe in eradication." This is like an old lady that Bud Robison once spoke of, who could not eat sheep, but she

loved mutton. To believe in a pure heart and not
in eradication is a contradiction. If sin is not eradicated, it is there; if it is there the heart is not pure;
if it is not pure we are coming short of the New Testament requisite.

Someone has defined dirt as "mater out of place."
The writer was recently walking down a depot plat-
form, and in so doing passed close to a large locomo-
tive. The engineer had just finished oiling the various
parts of the huge "iron horse," oil was dripping from
various parts down upon the ground. "That looks fine
there," we remarked to a friend, "that is just where
the oil belongs." But how would you like to have
some of it on your new gray suit? Oh! that is different, it would be out of place there. If dirt is "matter out of place" then sin, carnality, the old man, is
dirt, for it is entirely out of place in a pure heart, a
heart in which a holy God is to live. Everything
in the heart that is not in harmony with God's will is
"matter out of place" and must be labeled uncleanness
and not allowed to occupy a heart that is pure.

In conclusion, we call the reader's attention to the
fact that circumcision is one of the outstanding types
of sanctification. Circumcision as a type only serves
to emphasize the fact that cleansing, *and not suppression,* is the scriptural remedy for the sin problem. Circumcision, humanly performed, consisted in complete
parting, or doing away with; and when divinely performed we have not a single reason to assume that it
means anything less or different. Spiritual circumcision, therefore, consists of a complete separating or

taking away of "the body of sin." It is a circumcision of the heart not made with hands (Deut. 30:6; Col. 2:9, 11; Rom. 2:28, 19; Jer. 4:4).

God has in every age required that His children shall be separated from sin, and sin separated from them, that they be a holy people. Certainly a holy people necessitates the eradication of sin. Sin remaining in the heart in any capacity forever disqualifies it for holiness. The absence of sin means holiness, and the absence of holiness can only be attributed to the presence of sin. There can be no personal holiness without the eradication of sin. Thank God! He has made adequate provision, and "the blood of Jesus Christ his Son cleanseth us from all sin."

CHAPTER VIII

WHEN IS IT OBTAINED?

There is a rule in logic which declares, and it often so happens, that two proven facts will make the third fact self evident; in which case no argument is required to establish a proof, which is a logical conclusion of the two preceding established facts, as they prove themselves the third. For instance, we say, "Vegetation cannot grow without moisture." This is fact No. 1. Now we proceed to fact No. 2, and say, "Here is vegetation growing in abundance." Now here are two established facts beyond controversy; first, the fact that vegetation cannot grow without moisture; second, the fact that vegetation *is* growing. Now inasmuch as vegetation cannot grow without moisture, and furthermore, inasmuch as it is growing; the third fact is self-evident, namely: this vegetation has had moisture; this fact having been established by the two preceding ones.

Proceeding then upon the basis of this syllogism, we would investigate the matter of when the experience of sanctification is to be obtained. Syllogistically, let us state the case as follows: The two premises, or propositions, being the fact that we are born in sin, and the fact that no sin can ever enter heaven. These two premises make the conclusion self evident, namely, that somewhere between the time we are born, or otherwise become involved or entangled with sin, and the time we enter heaven's gate we must settle the sin question and find a solution for our deliverance.

Inbred sin, or inward depravity, is that sinful nature which is the result of the natural order of generation. As one writer declares, "It is the bitter root, of which actual sins are the bitter fruits. It is the natural evil tendency of the human heart in our fallen condition. It is the being of sin which lies back of the doing of sin. It is that within us which says no to God and yes to Satan. It exists in every human being that comes into the world as a bias or proclivity to evil. It is called in the New Testament, "the flesh," "the old man," "the body of sin," "sin that dwelleth in me," and the simple term sin in the sigular number.

Now to establish the first proposition of our syllogism, namely, that we are born in sin. We call the reader's attention, to begin with, that a continual effect must necessarily be preceded by a prevailing cause. When the world can be searched over, and in every clime, among all nations, and with people of various customs manners and habits, and with entirely different environment and training, there can never be found a single person, who is mentally responsible, that would say he had never sinned; isn't it plainly evident that this universal effect must be produced by a prevailing cause? This cause cannot be, in the very nature of the case, the individual's personality, habits, training or geographical location; for regardless of all these, they all possess the one general and universal moral weakness, the bias toward sin, insomuch that "all have sinned and come short of the glory of God" (Rom. 3:23). Now if the prevailing cause is not in personality, in environment, geographical location, customs or habits; where and in what can be found the solution to this universal weakness?

There is only one reasonable and logical answer, and it is also scriptural. It is to be found in the fact that we are all *by nature* the children of wrath (Eph. 2:3). The universality of sin is seen on every hand. The veracity of man is questioned everywhere. This is seen in the distrust of one for another. Everything must be watched; the boss watches the employee, and the proprietor watches the boss; the street car conductor rings up the fare as a testimony that the company which employs him holds him in question; the merchant's cash register also takes the witness stand and testifies to the fact that there is the old question mark, regardless of training or environment. There are many things on every hand that constantly advertise the fact that men unseasoned by grace are uncertain.

That we are by nature the children of wrath, and that the natural man without grace is sinful we believe can be easily demonstrated both by reason and revelation. It is often assumed by theologians that the human soul comes by direct creation, and is sometimes referred to by poets as the spark of Deity. We hold this a false assumption and out of harmony with nature and revelation. Wrapped up in every capsule, bound up in every kernel, packed up in every germ, is the written law of the Almighty, "Everything after *its kind*." According to this inexorable law, fallen humanity shall bring forth after their kind, hence the psalmist says, "Behold I was shapen in iniquity and in sin did my mother conceive me." If the soul were by direct creation, then your children would be no kin to you, for the body is but dust and the mere house in which the individual or personal being lives. The soul is the real man. In the course of a life-time the body changes many times, but we always retain our personality and individuality. If the soul is the real man, and comes by direct creation, then I am no kin to Adam, and the human race would not be one, but a conglomorated mass of beings, each having a separate origin. If on the other hand these individuals were sinful, then God would be guilty of creating sinners. Proof that sinful men are the posterity of Adam may be seen from the following scriptures: Rom. 5:12; Gen. 8:21; Jer. 17:9; Eph. 2:3; Rom. 7:20; and many others.

A further proof of the universal nature of sin in man may be seen in the universal nature of the atonement: "Jesus tasted death for every man," and God's promises are always made so as to include "the families *and their little ones*." The covenant of which circumcision was the seal, is an evidence that children were in a state of pollution. The universality of physical death is indicative of the fact that all are sinful; babies die as well as old folks, therefore babies are carnal, or else we have the ridiculous absurdity of the children suffering the effect without possessing the cause. These are a few of the outstanding evidences that we are by the natural order of generation the fallen creatures of a fallen ancestry.

Now concerning the second proposition, namely, that no sin can enter heaven; we are convinced there is only one source of authority upon this matter, that is the word of Him who holds the destiny of us all in His hand; all other statements at the best are only speculative. God speaks not with uncertainty but as one who knows. Such Scriptures as Psa. 24:3, 4; Heb. 12:14; Rev. 21:27; Gal. 5:19, 21, and others of like significance surely teach that sin can never enter into the abode of God, or we fail to understand the English language.

If these two premises are true, that is, that we are by nature sinful, and that no sin can enter heaven; it is evident upon the strength of these two facts that somewhere between the time we enter the world sinful and the time we enter heaven holy, we must have deliverance from the malady of sin, or none will ever be qualified to enter heaven. The sincere inquirer after light upon the subject and the faithful follower of Christ wants to know the truth and wants to be the best Christian he, or she, can possibly be, through the possibilities of divine grace.

The writer has no ax to grind, no favors to ask, no theological doctrine to defend, nor preference to manifest, any more than the fact that we want to know the truth. Jesus Christ once said, "And ye shall know the truth and the truth shall make you free." We want the philosophical, logical and scriptural solution to the problem regardless of our own personal likes or dislikes.

Investigation of this matter has led us to the conclusion that there are five outstanding theories relative to when it is obtainable: the purgatorial theory, the death theory, the growth theory, the conversion theory and the second work theory. We purpose to examine each one of these briefly and without partiality. We will take them in the order named:

The purgatorial theory is usually associated with the teaching of the Roman Catholic church; but we are aware of the fact that many Protestants are likewise banking on some sort of a post mortem salvation, to give the divine requisite for heaven. We are opposed to a post mortem provision, for several reasons, all of which we believe are reasonable and Scriptural. If there is a post mortem provision, whether it is purgatorial fire, or other means, whatever the means employed may be, in purifying our souls and giving us that holiness without which no man shall see the Lord; that which qualifies us for heaven, and is the means of deliverance from sin is in fact our savior. If a post mortem provision is to save us from sin, then whatever that provision is, it is in fact our savior instead of Jesus Christ. This theory takes the honor and glory that is due the precious blood of Christ and transfers it to some post mortem provision. This is a scriptural contradiction for the Word says, *"The blood of Jesus Christ his Son cleanseth us from all sin."* If, therefore, the blood cleanseth us from *all* sin, what need have we of further provision. If the blood cleanseth us from all sin, it is not true that purgatorial fire is the purifier. This would contradict the statement of

Holy Writ which says, "Wherefore Jesus also, *that he might sanctify* the people with his own blood, suffered without the gate." We realize, however, that sanctification is not confined to one instrument of execution. We are sanctfied by God the Father (Jude 1); we are sanctified by Jesus the Son, (Heb. 13:12); we are sanctified by the Holy Ghost (Rom. 15:16); sanctified through the truth (John 17:17); and sanctified by faith (Acts 15:8,9); thus we have the Father, the Son, the Holy Ghost, the truth, the blood, and faith as instruments in bringing this experience to pass. It is the gift of God, bought by the precious blood of Jesus, executed by the Holy Ghost, through the truth, that is the truth is the source of our knowledge, and the basis of our faith, and faith and consecration are the human conditions of its reception. J. A. Wood, in his, "Perfect Love," says, "The efficacious meritorious ground of purity is the atoning blood of Christ; the proximate conditional source of purity is faith; the instrumental source is the Word of God; and the grand efficient agent is the Holy Ghost." All these instruments have their part in purifying the souls of men; but it is never stated that purgatorial fire, or any other post mortem provision is the ground or instrument of our sanctification.

If the writer is rightly informed in this matter, holiness by the purgatorial route is entirely too expensive and uncertain a method, as one is forced to depend upon the prayers of an often too faithless minister, whose financial demands for their services are beyond the means of their parishioners. The writer is too poor to go that way and chooses to put the matter of his salvation in the hands of more reliable and responsible sources, rather than trust it to those who are as weak or weaker than himself. Reader, let Jesus Christ, who is the one mediator between God and man, be your Savior and also your Sanctifier; He is adequate to all you need.

The next theory, which is the death theory, is like the purgatorial theory in one respect at least, and that is, it robs the experience of all present tense value, for if we do not receive it until we die or in some post mortem provision, it is worth nothing to us here at all. It also, like the purgatorial theory, takes the honor and glory that should be ascribed to the Savior and transfers it to death. This placing the matter of sanctification beyond this present world, takes from it all its lifetime benefits, and defeats the very objective of the plan of salvation, which seems to have been that of making men holy in this world (Eph. 1:4; Gal. 1:4; Luke 1:73, 75).

If death is the sanctifier then all moral responsibility concerning this matter is removed for we have no moral responsibility relative to death. If death is the sanctifier then death is our savior instead of Jesus Christ, for that which delivers us from sin and gives us that holiness "without which no man shall see the Lord," is our savior. It furthermore confines the experience only to those who pass through the ordeal of death. Enoch, who walked with God, and Elijah, the brave prophet of old, and they which are alive and shall be caught up, will forever be deprived of the experience of sanctification because they did not die. If death is the sanctifier, then we should worship death instead of Jesus Christ. Death is nowhere mentioned in the scripture as a means of any work of grace. Death separates the soul from the body, but there is no indication, anywhere, to the effect that it can separate sin from the soul, and he who puts this task upon the ministry of death confers upon it a ministry that is nowhere substantiated either by reason or revelation. Other agencies are mentioned as being instruments of our sanctification, the Father, the Son, the Holy Ghost, the truth, the blood, but never is a word said about death as the agent of our purification; on the contrary, Peter says, "Seeing ye have purified your souls," how? By death? No. But by "obeying the truth through the spirit." If therefore death is not the instrument used and other means are used, why are they not efficient now, as later, or at the time of death? If the Holy Spirit can sanctify an hour before we die, why not now?

Furthermore the death theory makes the mattter unconditional and universal. Unconditional because we have no moral responsibility concerning death, and universal, because it is appointed unto man once to die. If death would sanctify one, it must sanctify all; anyone who dies, therefore, is assured of the divine fitness to see God regardless of his choice in the matter. To go a step farther it puts the whole matter of salvation upon a different basis from that which is clearly taught in the Book. God's declaration is that whosoever will, but if death is the sanctifier, then not only will the "whosoever wills" be sanctified, but the "whosoever won'ts" as well. This theory destroys the free moral agency of man altogether concerning salvation.

May we submit to the reader the question: How are we going *to serve God in holiness and righteousness all the days of our life,* if we do not receive it until we die? This is the privilege of the children of God, as revealed in Luke 1:73, 75. The apostle Paul says, "The very God of peace sanctify you *wholly,* and I pray God your whole spirit, soul and body be preserved blameless." Whatever this sanctification is, it is clearly set forth as a possibility before death, for it was to preserve us spirit, soul *and body;* consequently, it was for us while we were yet in the body. Inasmuch as death is a dissolution of the soul and body, it is evident that the sanctification for which he prays is for us in this present world, while we are yet inhabiting the physical body.

In the epistle to the Romans the apostle has the same idea. He says, "Knowing this that our old man is crucified with him, that the body of sin might be destroyed; that henceforth we should not serve sin." Notice, he does not say that the object of this crucifixion is that we may be immediately transported to heaven, but that "henceforth we should not serve sin." Thank God! This sanctification is not a dreamy ideal of a vague imagination, but is a vital and practical part of Christian experience. The objective, therefore, of the crucifixion of the old man is that we should not serve sin.

It is hardly possible that any rational or responsible Bible student would class sin as a friend or a thing desirable. We all agree that sin is an enemy. The Scripture has declared, however, that death is the last enemy that shall be destroyed; if this is true then sin, unless classed as a friend, must be destroyed before death. If we are not sanctified until we die, then all the Scripture that has relation to this experience is addressed to the dead and not the living. Why not carry the matter a step farther and say we are *justified* by death rather than faith, for there is as much reason to believe the one as there is to assume the other. If death will sanctify, why will it not justify?

"But," says the objector, "we do not believe that death is the sanctifier. We believe that the Holy Spirit sanctifies at the hour of death." Very well then, if the Holy Spirit has to do the work after all; if eventually, why not now? Why can the Holy Spirit not do it as well now as at some future time? "Oh," you say, "but when we are dying we can better meet the conditions, for we are willing to give up all." All right then, bring yourself to absolute surrender to God, giving up everything to Him just as you would if you were dying, and God will surprise you by giving you sanctification (dying grace) to enable you to live the life of a more than conqueror. Reader, there is no evidence that God will be more willing or able to sanctify you at some future time than He is now. Now is always the accepted time with God. If you are to advocate the sanctification of believers on their death beds, why not advocate the conversion of sinners the same way?

We come next to a theory of holiness which has a very large following, that is, the theory of growth into sanctification. The person who talks about growing into holiness or sanctification shows that he is lacking in proper conception as to what it is.

Whatever definition may be given to sanctification, whether it be consecration, to set apart, to purify or make holy, to consecrate to a sacred purpose; in fact, no sensible defining of the word will permit of the possibility of growing into it. One could not grow into consecration, for that is an act of human volition; one could not grow into "being set apart," neither could one grow into purity, because purity is a process of subtraction, while growth is a process of addition. The very nature of sanctification is such that it cannot be obtained by growth. Purity is instantaneous and complete. Some adjectives and adverbs which denote perfection of quality admit of no comparison. There is no sense in saying, round, rounder, roundest, or square, squarer, squarest. If it is less than round it is not round, if it is less than square it is not square, if it is round or square it can be no more than that, for less than that disqualifies it to be round or square. When a thing is pure, it can be no purer than pure, while to be less than pure, is to be impure. Purity admits of no degrees, but growth does. If sanctification is the result of growth, death, works, human efforts, education, will power, discipline or anything else, than what it is, Jesus need not have died to bring it to pass (Heb. 13:12, 14).

Sanctification is a cleansing and therefore cannot be obtained by growth, for cleansing is a process of subtraction while growth is a process of addition; one is a taking away and the other is an adding to. It would be ridiculous to talk about one's hands or face growing clean; yet it is no more absurd to speak of this than to suppose one's heart would grow clean. Furthermore, we must not confuse maturity with purity. Sanctification is not maturity, it is only purity. Maturity is the result of growth, it is addition; but purity is the result of cleansing, that is, a taking away and is subtraction. Growth is the gradual development of a nature as it is. The law of growth is stated in Genesis, "everything after his kind." Six thousand years have failed to give a single exception to this rule. Growth implies an increase of quantity, but not a change in nature. Sin can never grow into holiness. The object of sanctification is to get rid of sin, to purify the heart. You can no more grow sin out of the heart than you can grow rotten out of an apple.

Instantaneous sanctification is the only kind that will meet our need. Anyone of us who are living today may be dead tomorrow; if, therefore, sanctification is to be by growth, time is a factor and the question naturally arises, how much time? If time is a factor we may have to die without it, seeing we may die today. "But," says the objector, "in that case God would finish the work; his Holy Spirit would cleanse the soul." Very well, if after all the Holy Spirit is to do the work, *why not let him do it now?* The world needs the influence of pure hearts to season its moral rottenness, and it is Satan's big camouflage of procrastination that has kept many who otherwise might have enjoyed the blessing from having it, by telling them it must be attained by a long process of development. Isaiah's blessing was not developed, but delivered. Satan would steal your present blood bought privilege by making you believe it is yet a long way off. The reader may have it now, if he will meet the conditions and exercise the faith.

A German philosopher says, "The notion of progress contains of necessity that of an object, for if after having taken a thousand steps, I am no nearer the goal than before I started to walk, because it ever remains infinitely removed from me, such progress in reality is no progress at all." This is the outstanding failure in the growth theory of sanctification. It is universally observed that those who advocate the growth theory of sanctification are always in pursuit and never in possession of their objective. The writer has heard thousands of people testify to the experience of sanctification; but we have yet to hear our first witness who would declare that he was in possession of the experience, and that he received it by the process of growth. The growth advocates are ever on the road but never reaching their destination. We are by no means alone in this opinion. Mr. Wesley says, "In London alone I found six hundred and fifty-two members of our society who were exceeding clear in their experience, and of whose testimony I could see no reason to doubt . . . . and every one of these (after a most careful inquiry, I have not found *one exception* either in Great Britain or Ireland) has declared that his deliverance from sin was instantaneous; that the change was wrought in a moment. Had half of these or one-third, or one in twenty, declared it was gradually wrought in them, I should have believed this in regard to them, and thought that some wre gradually sanctified, and some instantaneously. But as I have not found in so long a space of time (thirty years) a single person speaking thus; as all who believe they are sanctified declare with one voice that the change was wrought in a moment; I cannot but believe that sanctification is commonly if not always an instantaneous work," (Wesley Sermons, Vol. 2, page 223).

Let the reader not misunderstand us and think that we are opposed to growing in grace; not so. We believe and strongly advocate growing in grace; but we must not fail to discriminate in the matter of growing *in* grace and that of growing *into* grace. Sanctification does not end growth; but cleanses the heart from the antagonistic elements that would hinder growth. Growth plants no new quality in the growing matter, it only develops the properties belonging to its substance. If we could grow out of regeneration into sanctification; we could just as consistently grow out of sin into regeneration. Sanctification, like regeneration, is a mighty operation of the Spirit of God upon the soul, and is the gift of God. Gifts are bestowed upon, and not grown into. You do not grow into a gift, you receive it definitely, personally and instantaneously.

The very nature of the work of sanctification is such that it is impossible to obtain it by growth. Sanctification is an act, a grace freely given, merely this and nothing more; it is not the fruit of a long and perilous journey toward heaven; it is not trying nor suffering, nor resolving, nor achieving, but a simple reaching out by the hand of faith and taking. May we not ask what is there in a gift that necessitates a long period of time for its reception; or what is there in a cleansing that would require years of growth to receive?

Summing up the whole matter of being sanctified by growth, our objections in a nutshell are, first: We have tested it many times in crowds and have our first person yet to find who will testify to the possession of the experience, who will acknowledge that he received it by growth. Second: The growth people do not only fail to receive it themselves but they fail to get anyone else into the experience. A doctor that never cured a patient, a lawyer that never won a case, a farmer that never raised a crop, we would count a failure; likewise a doctrine that never produces a concrete example of its theory is a failure. Third: The Bible does not sustain it. Fourth: The nature of the experience does not permit it. Fifth: The preachers and laymen that endorse this theory never preach about it, nor write about it, nor make any effort otherwise to get anybody into the experience. Their chief stock in trade is their criticism of those who have been more successful than themselves. The writer has known many who have forsaken the false and unsuccessful theory of growth, and found the blessed grace of heart purity, through consecration and faith instantaneously. "The proof of the pudding is the eating of it." The doctrine that produces the results and makes the seekers happy finders is the one, and only one that is a success. Sixth: If it is by faith it is not by growth; and if by faith why is time required? Seventh: Growth is human development, but sanctification is the gift of God. Let the reader not be deprived of the present privileges of this blessing by adopting this erroneous idea of growth, or other long drawn out processes, that will rob the experience of all its present values.

We now come to the theory of sanctification at conversion. We have often heard it said, "I got *it* at conversion." The very fact that they specify *it* as distinct from conversion, is an acknowledgment of the fact that *it* is not conversion, but something else. But did they really get *it* at conversion? If sanctification is wrought in the heart simultaneous with conversion and accompanies conversion, then everyone who is converted is sanctified, and likewise all who are not sanctified are not converted. "If men are sanctified when they are converted," says one writer, "then the Christian Church is to be reduced from millions to units; for if this doctrine is correct we must count as converted only those who are sanctified." "It is well to remember" says Rev. B. Carradine, D. D., "that Christ calls regeneration a new birth, and it is a spiritual birth as He represents it to be; and is not and cannot be a crucifixion. There is a striking difference in the two figures. We could never understand spiritual things if God presented them in such a hopeless irreconcilable language. A cradle and a cross are two distinct and widely different things; likewise a birthday and a death. You never saw a man get in a cradle, and you never beheld the grewsome spectacle of a baby being crucified."

It seems that the "get-it-at-conversion" theologians' principal object is to do away with that objectionable feature of a "second blessing." This however, would be a difficult matter to accomplish as the two works, justification and sanctification, are distinctly different in their meaning and relation to Christian experience, consequently, if both were obtained at once, it would be two distinct and separate things, simultaneously received, and thus be two separate works. If we are converted and sanctified at the same time, then sanctification is for sinners, and if this is their privilege, they should be told of it. But alas, those who get it all at conversion never say anything about it, unless someone comes along advocating the second blessing theory, and then to the surprise of everybody they confess that they have had it all the time; or worse yet, get peeved at the "second blessing" advocates and show by their conduct that they are mistaken in getting it at all.

The writer offers two objections to the conversion theory. First: It is contrary to the experience and testimony of the major part of professing Christians. Second: It is not in harmony with the Scriptural teaching upon the matter. That it is contrary to Christian experience and testimony we have demonstrated too often to doubt. We have often asked the question in public congregations, "How many are sanctified?" only to find a decided minority respond. We have then asked the question, of the same congregation, "How many are Christians, but not sanctified?" and always found a decidedly larger number respond to that inquiry. Either the majority have received it at conversion, without ever knowing it, or else they did not receive it at all. If they received it at conversion it was received without seeking it, without asking for it, or without the exercise of faith, all of which are in contradiction to the facts as revealed in the Word of God. Is it possible that the highest standard of grace in the New Testament could be conferred upon a soul, and that individual never discover that such a remarkable work of grace had been accomplished?

Dr. Adam Clarke, the great commentator says, "I have been twenty-three years a traveling preacher, and have been acquainted with some thousands of Christians during that time who were in different states of grace, and I never to my knowledge met a single instance where God both justified and sanctified at the same time."

There are some confusing and inextricable difficulties in this idea of justification and sanctification being at the same time. Says Rev. J. A. Wood, "If sanctification is complete at justification then every man who enjoys religion is sanctified. If sanctification is complete at conversion, then every Christian, to be truthful, should profess sanctification. If all who are converted are entirely sanctified, then all the directions in the Word of God to seek holiness, sanctification, or perfect love, are given exclusively to sinners. If justification and sanctification are inseparable, then all who feel the fruits of the flesh are in a state of condemnation." (This would disqualify them from being Christians at all, for there is no condemnation to them that are in Christ Jesus.) "If sanctification is complete at conversion then everybody who is not sanctified is a child of the devil."

Says the Rev. G. D. Watson, D. D., for many years an expositor of rare ability, and a man of remarkable spiritual insight, "The scriptures teach that in conversion one is always sanctified or purified back to the moral cleanness of infancy. This is the exact limit of partial sanctification, which is fixed by the Savior himself, 'Except ye be converted and become as little children.' Just as pardon removes all guilt resulting from actual transgression, so the washing of regeneration removes all the impurity acquired by actual transgression. The removal of remaining original impurity is the work of entire sanctification."

One thing we must not overlook is this, that the advocates of this theory are the least productive of the fruits of their doctrine. They never preach it, never testify to it, never lead anybody into the experience of entire sanctification, and are usually notorious in their opposition and antagonism to anyone else's either professing or possessing it. It seems to the writer that since they were so fortunate in receiving this great grace when they were converted, they ought to publish the glad news, for if sanctification is for sinners they ought to know it and have it, but "shades of theology," they are so silent and dumb about the matter that if the world was dependent upon them for light upon the subject, it would live forever in darkness. About the only time they ever mention such a thing as sanctification is when a "second blessing" preacher comes around and stirs them up on the question; then to the surprise of everyone they are *provoked* to confess that they have had it all the time. Perhaps their silence about the matter is due to the same reason that some Christians have for not wanting to do personal work: there is a sense of lack in themselves.

"But why," says the objector, "cannot God sanctify us at the time of our conversion?" We presume if it were merely a matter of physical omnipotence God could do many things that He does not. We must not lose sight of the fact that the plan of salvation is based upon the free moral agency of man. The promise of God is always to the whosoever will. It may be further stated that everything that is received in the realms of grace is based upon our faith to receive it. "According to your faith" is always the basis of our receiving from God either temporal or spiritual blessing. To execute an intelligent faith, we must have a knowledge of the truth; hence faith cometh by hearing, and hearing by the Word of God. It would be physically and morally impossible to intelligently exercise faith for something about which, perhaps, you have never heard, or never known anything about; therefore the degree of our light is the ground of our faith, and the measure of our faith the measure by which we are to receive.

Upon this point the Rev. Asbury Lowery, D. D., says, "As already stated herein the work of sanctification and justification, or conversion, are so distinctly different in their nature, and can by no means be made to refer to the same thing; that is if both experiences were received simultaneously, the reader would have received two seperate and distinct works of grace; and would thus not be able to eliminate the objectionable feature of the second work. In the first place God always saves in proportion to our ability or preparation to receive. God would not try to put the Atlantic Ocean in the Mississippi River. He wisely adapts His bestowments according to our capacity or ability to receive them. He must therefore confer upon us according to the light we have." Light is an essential factor in the plan of salvation; we can receive only in the degree that we have light, and are only responsible accordingly. It is a rare thing (if ever) that we find a sinner in the darkness of spiritual death who is able to comprehend the need of entire sanctification, or feel a desire for it. To receive this experience at the time of conversion would in 999 times out of 1,000 be to receive it without any light upon the subject, without an intelligent understanding of the need concerning it, which would therefore disqualify one to exercise an intelligent and grasping faith concerning the matter. We are perfectly willing that the reader shall have the blessing at the time of his conversion, if he can succeed in getting it that way, and we will rejoice with him in his gracious privilege; but we are frank to say that if he succeeds in this, he will receive it in a way contrary to the testimony and experience of evangelical orthodox Christianity, and contrary to any case on record, either in the Old or New Testament.

But now in conclusion let us submit to the reader the fact, that after being a student of the Bible for more than twenty years, we do not know of a single case on record where a new convert was baptized with the Holy Spirit, or sanctified, at the time of his conversion. On the other hand we are able to introduce to the reader many who received this gracious experience after they were disciples of the Lord Jesus Christ. May we give one instance. Jesus in the seventeenth chapter of John is praying for His disciples, and He says, "Sanctify them." Would He pray for them to receive what they already possessed? But lest the reader say they were not converted, we call your attention to the fact that *"none of them were lost."* This is a clear statement as to their being saved, for one cannot be saved and lost both, nor can he be neither saved nor lost. The fact that none of them were lost is equivalent to saying they were saved. The reader may object and say that they were saved once but had backslidden. Jesus settled that matter by saying, "I have kept them" (Jno. 17:12).

If the reader will turn to Jno. 1:11, 12, he will find the fact of discipleship is based upon two fundamental principles, namely, *believing and receiving*. "As many *as received him, to them* gave he power to become the sons of God." To whom? To as many as *received Him.* What did He do? Gave them the power to become the sons of God. Even to *them that believed* on His name. To those that did what? To those *that believed on* Him. Here are the two principles of discipleship, *receiving and believing*. Were these for whom He prayed able to measure up to this requisite of discipleship? Let the reader turn now again to Jno. 17:8, and you will find that those for whom He was praying, had conformed to these very two fundamental requisites, that is, they had *believed and received*. "I have given unto them the words which thou gavest me; and they have *received* them, and have known surely that I came out from thee, and they have *believed* that thou didst send me" (Jno. 17:8). Thus these for whom He prays had believed and received, and in so doing according to the scriptural standard had qualified as disciples. The question of their sonship is established. Is it possible that the Son of God would make the stupid blunder of praying for these disciples to receive what they already possessed; having received it when they were saved (for none of them were lost). If Jesus knew the facts as they were, they surely did not receive sanctifying grace when they became disciples, or else the Holy Spirit is guilty of a stupid blunder in inspiring such a prayer, and Jesus was woefully mistaken in praying for them to receive after their conversion what they had already received when they were saved.

May the reader never be gulled into discounting anything that God has written for our edification and profit; if God has declared that it is His will even our sanctification, and that Jesus suffered without the gate that He might sanctify us with His own blood; the least we can do is to make an effort to know and possess this great grace. Do not quibble about a second work of grace, if you are converted and not sanctified, whether it is a second work for anyone else or not, *it will be for you* if you ever receive it.

If we are not sanctified by any post mortem provision, or by death, or growth, or at conversion, and we must have it to get to heaven, we are left with only one method of execution and that is by a specific work of grace subsequent to regeneration; a work of the Holy Spirit. We will discuss this in a following chapter.

CHAPTER IX

The "Second Blessing"

We approach the subject matter of this chapter conscious of the fact that we are dealing with a question concerning which there is much prejudice and misunderstanding. We believe as a writer upon the subject we are in a position to give to the reader a fair and unbiased interpretation of God's Word upon the subject. We are convinced that if a doctrine cannot be established without bending the Scripture to favor what one wishes to teach, such doctrine had better go untaught. If we are compelled to wrest the Scripture in order to make it support our theory, such interpretation is unworthy of intelligent consideration. No doubt some unwise teachers in their desire to support the doctrine of a second work of grace have made a mistake in using scriptures that have no bearing upon the subject whatsoever, in an effort to establish their claim. If the doctrine of a second work of grace cannot be proven without stretching the imagination and bending the scriptures out of their rightful significance, it had better go unproven. Never try to bend God's Word to make it teach what you want to believe, but shape your doctrines to conform to the "thus saith the Lord."

But we ask, as a matter of fact, does regeneration and consequent justification place a man in the

THE "SECOND BLESSING" 111

experience of sanctification? Does one work of grace
lead us into finished Christianity (aside of course from
development of Christian character)? Does regeneration mean that a man possesses the fullness of the
blessing of the gospel of Christ? Are regeneration
and sanctification relative terms? Are they to be
understood as referring to the same experience in
grace? Is everybody who is justified, sanctified? Is
there such a thing as a work of grace after we are
converted?

The writer believes there are abundant scriptures
to sustain the doctrine of a second spiritual crisis, without in the least way whatsoever wresting or misinter-
preting the Word. We submit two or three of the
many. We are sure that Jesus Christ died for sinners;
but we are equally sure that He also died for our
sanctification (Heb. 13:12, 13; Eph. 5:25, 27). That
sanctification of believers is the ultimate objective
of the plan of salvation may be seen from such scriptures as Eph. 1:4; 2 Thes. 2:13, and others. It is also
clear to the careful observer that conversion is not
finished Christianity. In the very nature of the two
terms, regeneration and sanctification, they do not
mean the same thing, and do not sustain the same relation to Christian experience. Regeneration has to do
with the giving of spiritual life to those who are dead
in trespasses and in sins. "And you hath he quickened, who were dead in trespasses and in sins," says
the apostle. This operation of the Holy Spirit gives
to us life and light, it is the planting in the soul the
elixir of spiritual life. Sanctification is the cleansing

from the soul all the native inherent sin. One is the giving of a new or spiritual nature, the other is the taking away of an old or sinful nature.

Regeneration generally and properly speaking has relation to the new birth, being born again spiritually; though it is sometimes used in a more comprehensive sense so as to include sanctification or the restoration of the whole man to the image of God. It is correct to say that a man is regenerated if he is sanctified, but it is not always true to say that he is sancitified because he is regenerated. Upon this point the Rev. Jesse T. Peck, D. D., well says, "The scriptures conclusively settle the question. They plainly assume the distinction. To sinners God says, 'Ye must be born again.' To the regenerate He says, 'As he which hath called you is holy, *so be* ye holy'" The number who have been renewed in the whole man after the image of God are comparatively few compared to the number that profess to be Christians. Indeed the number is small who profess to be wholly sanctified; but are we to assume that these are the only Christians in the world, and the rest are all hypocrites? This is not true, and he who would sweep away at a single stroke so great a part of Christendom, has surely not given reasonable and scriptural investigation to the subject. And yet he who asserts that we are sanctified when we are converted, unchristianizes all who do not claim to be sanctified.

The identity of the Church may be established upon the basis of a certain quality of moral and spiritual integrity, and not upon our sectarian affiliations.

The Church is not undenominational; it is rather inter-
denominational; that is, it is made up of a certain
quality, regardless of our denominational associations.
What is this quality? It is the being born again.
By virtue of that work of grace, we automatically become a member of *the* Church. In other
words, the Church is composed of regenerated people.
There are often unregenerated people in the various
denominations; but to be in the Scriptural Church, we
must be born again. Upon this basis of interpretation
concerning the Church let us observe that Christ is rep-
resented as so loving this institution that He gave
himself for it (Eph. 5:25, 27). What was the purpose of this phase of the sacrificial offering of Jesus?
To sanctify and cleanse. Cleanse whom? The Church.
Who is the Church? Those who have been born
again, or regenerated. If this is a correct analysis
of the identity of the Church, then Jesus gave Himself
to sanctify and cleanse those that were born again.

The apostle prays elsewhere for the entire sanctification of the Thessalonians when he says, "The very
God of peace sanctify you wholly." There have been
some who have tried to make it appear as if this church
was in a deplorable condition, and needed reclamation
rather than sanctification. Hear what the apostle has
to say of their spiritual condition. He says, "We give
thanks to God always for you all." Does the reader
imply that he was giving thanks to God for them because they were in a deplorable spiritual condition?
If so you can well change your opinion on reading a
little further when says, "Remembering without ceas-

ing *your work of faith, your labor of love, and patience of hope in our Lord Jesus Christ;* knowing brethren beloved, *your election of God.* For our gospel came not to you in word only, but also in power, and in the Holy Ghost, and in *much assurance;* and ye *became followers of us, and of the Lord;* having received the word in much affliction *and joy in the Holy Ghost;* so *that ye were ensamples* to all that believed in Macedonia and Achaia; *your faith to Godward is spread abroad;* and how ye turned from idols *to serve the living and true God."* We have given the reader here just a few scattered excerpts from the opening chapter of this epistle in order that we might have Paul's interpretation of the condition of this people for whom he prayed. Here are eight unmistakable evidences of the fact that they were converted people, yet he prays for them, "the very God of peace sanctify you wholly." A word of encouragement is also added in the twenty-fourth verse, that they may expect something which they did not yet possess; "faithful is he that calleth you who also *will do it"* (not has done it). Here is a sanctification for those who have eight badges of discipleship. Paul knew how to pray for the church according to their needs. Praying for reclamation he says, "Ye did run well, who did hinder you?" (Gal. 5:7). "I travail in birth for you *again"* (Gal. 4:19). Indeed he would never make the blunder of praying for backsliders to be sanctified. When he prays for disciples whose faith and devotion had made them examples, and who had turned from idols to serve the true and living God, he says, "and the very God of peace sanctify you wholly."

This language in verse twenty-three, states very clearly that the God of peace is to do the sanctifying, showing conclusively that it is for justified people, for they alone have peace with God, or a God of peace. "Therefore being justified by faith *we have peace* with God." If this sanctification is to be executed by a *God of peace,* it is likely that it is for those who have a God of peace. This is something that no sinner has; "There is no peace saith my God to the wicked." It may be logically concluded therefore, that the sanctification for which the apostle prays is for those who have been justified, or in the language of the text, those who have a God of peace. This excludes the sinner from the benefits of this prayer and brands him as ineligible for sanctification until he has first made peace with God, or has a God of Peace. Here then is sanctification, for justified people of sterling Christian character and quality, subsequent to their being initiated into discipleship.

We regret that we will not be able to go into detail relative to other scriptures such as Jno. 14:14, 15, where the Holy Spirit is promised to His disciples in a sense in which they *had not* yet received him and in a sense in which the world could not receive Him. In Acts 19:1, 6, where certain disciples had not yet received the Holy Ghost in a measure that it was their privilege to do, though they were disciples. Then there is Eph. 1:13. There must have been a peculiar something to which the apostle referred as the sealing of the Spirit, that was to take place after they had believed unto salvation.

A metaphorical confirmation of this truth may be found in John 15:1, 2. Here Jesus likens the Christian to a branch in the vine; man being the branch and He, himself being the vine. There are three kinds of branches mentioned in the text, one bearing no fruit, and the other bearing fruit, and one bearing more fruit. If fruit bearing is an indication of spiritual life, then we fear there are many lifeless branches encumbering the vine. But what about these branches? Hear ye the Word of the Lord. "Every branch in me *that beareth not fruit he taketh it away*"; in other words, fruit bearing is the test of discipleship. "Every branch in me that beareth not fruit is taken away." But what about the branches that do bear fruit? "He purgeth them that they may bring forth more fruit." The fact that the branch is bearing fruit is an acknowledgment that it possesses life; for fruit does not grow on dead branches. Here then is a living branch being purged. What is this purging? Webster defines it as being, "to cleanse or free from impurities or guilt." At any rate, to adhere to the figure of the vine, it is a process of subtraction. If this metaphor does not suggest a cleansing for the living branch in the vine, a process of taking away, and if this living branch in the vine is not to be interpreted as a true disciple of our Lord, pray what is the meaning of these words of Jesus?

Every child of Abraham's blood was an heir of

Canaan, and every Spirit born child of grace is an heir to the spiritual Canaan, the baptism of the Holy Spirit, or sanctification. You cannot be an heir until you are born; neither can dead people inherit anything. It is the live children that are heirs. Sinners are dead and must be born again, made alive, before they can be heirs to sanctification.

In all ages and in all Christian lands, always and everywhere, soon after men are converted they are conscious of an inward antagonism to the will of God. While they have passed from death unto life, they also find themselves in the midst of a conflict with an inward foe, as Paul calls it, "the old man," "the sin that dwelleth in me." Now as one writer puts it, "One of three things must be true. First, either all these must be mistaken in calling themselves regenerated, or second, they have all backslidden, or third, they are truly regenerate while struggling with the carnal nature. To assert the first is to assert that the whole Christian world is deceived relative to their conversion. To assert the second is to admit the backsliding of its members soon after their conversion. The third alternative saves the church from deception on the one hand and apostasy on the other; and is in perfect harmony with God's Word, and universal testimony of orthodox Christianity.

It is plainly evident that from the plan God uses in the physical world, he is a God of order and system. It is not likely that a God who has adhered so strictly to a system in the natural or physical world would discard all systematic plan when it comes to the solution of moral and spiritual problems. No doubt He has adopted a plan or policy in the redemptive scheme for man. As to why God does or does not do certain things it is sometimes difficult to say. Sometimes His providences are mysterious indeed. There are some things, however, upon which we need not speculate when the fact itself has become so generally conceded. No one asks why the sun does not rise in the west; no one ever asks why God did not put the Rocky Mountains in Indiana instead of Colorado; no one ever debates upon a subject the fact of which is already settled beyond controversy. We may not always know the "why" of God's program, but the facts we can know. God planned before the foundation of the world to send His Son Jesus to save men; but why He waited four thousand years to do so we cannot know, other than to speculate. He promised the Holy Spirit, this we know, but why He waited fifty days to send Him we cannot know, except to speculate. Everywhere in the physical and spiritual realm may be seen the finger prints of design and purpose. Dawn before day, seed time before harvest, youth before age; and likewise in the spiritual God has His order of procedure.

It might have been possible for God to have sanctified His people, independent of any condition on their part; but inasmuch as He has seen fit to grant us this great grace upon conditions; it is unthinkable to suppose that He will grant the grace without the condition, and equally unthinkable to assume that such condition can be met without the necessary information and light upon the subject. If God is to save us according to our capacity to intelligently receive His grace; then it must be concluded that only those can be sanctified who have knowledge and light sufficient to give them a proper need of such an experience; and who have been taught the manner and condition of its reception.

Just how a man may have light and not perfect light upon his need may be illustrated, perhaps, by analogy. Did the reader ever sit in a room well lighted and apparently in tidy condition and well cleaned, only to discover when a ray of sunlight came streaming in the window it revealed a world of dirt particles and dust, that hitherto had been unseen? For some wise cause God has not seen fit to reveal all the hidden impurities of the heart before we are converted, lest perhaps in our weakness we become discouraged before we learn to lean upon the strong arm of One who is mighty to save. So it is in the life of the sinner, he receives light that he is able to comprehend; and if he walks in that light, more light will be given him, by which he may be able to see the hitherto hidden things of the inner man; and thus enable him to see the need of entire holiness or sanctification.

A distinguished writer upon this subject says, "In the new birth the tone, temper and tendency of our minds are changed, the current of our feelings is made to run in a different channel, and a capacity to do the will of God is imparted. But the holiness which is then realized is proportioned to our faith. If it be possible before regeneration to discover all the depravity of our nature in its diversified features and operations; if we are made thoroughly sensible of its presence, and are as much concerned for its removal as we are for the pardon of our guilt and the repeal of our condemnation; if in addition we have a faith proportional to such repentance; if faith which is not embarrassed by any doubt, but which covers over the vast extent of the broad commandment and the gracious promise of entire sanctification; we know no reason in the divine economy to prevent the fulfillment of that promise, so that we may be perfectly sanctified in the very moment when we are freely justified. But self knowledge so thorough, and faith so strong and extensive, securing sanctifying grace so prevailing, powerful and perfect are seldom, *if ever*, realized before we are born again."

When it comes to reducing the science of experimental sanctification to being obtained in conversion; it seems to be decidedly impractical for the following reasons. First, we did not expect it, and therefore did not seek it. Second, we did not understand its full significance and therefore did not feel our need of it. Third, knowing nothing of it, and failing to seek it, there was no faith exercised for its reception. Fourth, no faith being exercised for its reception and no effort being made to obtain it, it must be given unconditionally, so far as the seeker is concerned. Fifth, if received after this manner, it would be of no value to the recipient, having no knowledge of its possession, and no understanding of its purpose.

If the reader is converted and conscious of the fact he is not sanctified, let him not be satisfied until he has sought and found this pearl of great price. Sanctifying grace is the rightful privilege for the believer as truly as pardoning love is the privilege of the sinner.

CHAPTER X

How To Receive It

If the reader has followed us through the contents of this volume until now; surely he must be convinced that regeneration is not sanctification, or Christian perfection. Perhaps you are asking yourself, "Now that I am a Christian, how can I obtain this experience of entire sanctification?" May we submit to you, therefore, a simple rule of procedure toward obtaining this wonderful blessing.

First, the reader must desire the experience above everything else. There must be a hungering and thirsting after righteousness and a determination, at any price, by God's grace to possess it. A listless, half hearted effort to obtain it will never be rewarded with success. You must desire it with your whole heart. The universal testimony of those who have received it is to this effect. In fact, the unanimous testimony of those who are enjoying the experience is that preceding its reception there was an intense heart hunger for this grace. Hannah Whitehall Smith says, "My whole heart panted after entire conformity to the will of God." D. L. Moody said, "I came to that state, I think, where I would have died if I had not got it." Rev. B. Carradine, D. D., says, "I wanted perfect love to God and man." Dear reader, if you do not feel that you are concerned about this matter as you

should be, ask God to give you the needed heart cry
for His sanctifying grace. This is the first necessary
step.

Second, you must believe it is for you. No man
will likely ever seek an experience that he doubts is
possible. Unbelief concerning this matter is fatal to
your efforts to obtain it and disqualifies you to receive
anything from the Lord. When we come to God
we must believe that He is, and that He is a rewarder
of them that diligently seek Him; for without faith it
is impossible to please God. The promise is *to you*,
and you must be brought to a realization of that fact.
No Christian will ever obtain the experience until
he is persuaded that there is in reality such an experience, and that it is for him. You must, therefore,
bring yourself to a profound conviction that it is for
you, and not only a privilege but a necessity. Stimu-
late your faith with the promises of God. Peter said,
"The promise is to you and to your children, and to
them that are afar off, even as many as the Lord
your God shall call." Jesus says, "Neither pray I
for these alone, but for them also which shall believe on me through their word."

Having thus realized that it is scriptural, that it
is possible and that it is for you, you now become indeed a candidate for its reception. Accept every promise concerning it, therefore, as your promise, as literally as if you were the only person in the world for
whom the plan of salvation had been provided. Having
progressed thus far, one more preliminary step is in-
valuable to the seeker. He must not only believe that

there is such an experience, and that it is for him, but he must take another step and believe that it is for him now. Why should you delay? Is it not a fact that every delay is disastrous in spiritual things? God's time is always now. You have deprived yourself of the blessing personally, you have denied yourself the privilege of its enjoyment; but worse, you have robbed the church of the influence of a holy and Spirit-filled life and the efficient service of a member endued with power from on high, all because of your delay. It is costing you the rewards of a victorious, useful and Spirit-filled life every moment you procrastinate. Remember, reader, it is for you *now*. Unbelief at this point will certainly prevent your receiving, for you must ask nothing wavering.

Third, just as repentance and faith constitute the condition of regeneration, so consecration and faith compose the basis upon which sanctification is obtained. Where is the line to be drawn and what is the mark of distinction between repentance and consecration? Did we not surrender everything when we were converted? In a word, what is the difference between the consecration such as the Christian makes when seeking sanctification and the surrender that the sinner makes when he is seeking pardon? In defining the two terms, surrender and consecration, Webster's International says of surrender, "To give up one's self into the power of another." Concerning consecration, he says, "To make sacred, to set apart to a sacred purpose." It would seem, therefore, that while the act of yielding in itself is strikingly similar, the purpose of the two terms is entirely different. The yielding, also, of consecration is of a higher order than the surrender of a sinner. It is more intelligent, more comprehensive, and of a quality of which sinners are utterly incapable. We never expect a new convert to know what the more mature Christian knows, and the unregenerated sinner can never know what the man knows who has passed from death unto life and from darkness unto light. The heart illuminated by regenerating grace is capable of a fuller and more intelligent yielding to God than the sinner who is in spiritual darkness and the bondage of sin. The consecration of the Christian is made with a different purpose from the surrender of the sinner. The sinner surrenders seeking pardon and deliverance from the guilt and bondage of sin. He is fleeing the wrath to come and is asking for deliverance from condemnation. The Christian making a consecration is not under condemnation, for there is no condemnation to them that are in Christ Jesus. His conviction is for holiness, it is not a conviction of guilt, but rather a conviction of want, or need; a hungering after more of God, a heart cry for the fullness of God in the soul. It is a higher form of obedience of which Christians only are capable. As the sinner gives up all his wicked things and lays down his arms of rebellion, so the Christian gives all his ransomed being, presents himself a living sacrifice, to be devoted to the service and interest of God's kingdom forever.

As the poet puts it:

> Here I give my all to thee,
>   Friends and time, and earthly store,
> Soul and body thine to be
>   Wholly thine forever more."

One writer describing consecration says, "It is that act or disposition of ourselves toward God which puts us in an attitude to receive. It is the emptying of ourselves to be filled. It is the releasing of our hold upon everything, that God may have us and ours. It is the assignment of all our possessions, real or fancied, to Him for sacrifice or service. Consecration is an unreserved and irrevocable dedication of ourselves to God. It is in its nature somewhat similar to what we did in repentance, except that it is for a different purpose and with a fuller knowledge of our need than when we repented."

Consecration is more comprehensive than the surrender of a sinner, for it includes all our good things in life which were not given when we were giving up evil and sin to be converted. Nothing then was said about our good things. The penitent sinner gives himself to God that he may receive pardon; he knows little or nothing of the program of redemption or what God shall call upon him to do. He is asking only a cancellation of his guilt and wants to effect a reconciliation. He wants the burden of his transgressions lifted. As a result of his repentance, God gives him all he seeks, all he asks, all his faith believes for, and fully and completely justifies him. He soon finds, however, that he has not graduated in spiritual things, nor is his spiritual birth finished Christianity. He is soon brought to a sense of a greater need, the need of a deliverance from an inward antagonist, for the flesh lusteth against the spirit and the spirit against the flesh. In fact, he soon finds that he did not give himself to God for sanctification and did not realize at the time of his repentance his need of such a grace.

There may be rare cases where the sinner has had line upon line, and precept upon precept, until he is thoroughly indoctrinated, and before he comes to the altar as a seeker is conscious of his full need and can intelligently meet the required conditions for sanctification as well as regeneration. If there are such cases they are the exception to the rule. However, under such conditions, we doubt not, it would be possible to receive the experience of sanctification, providing the conditions upon which the blessing is to be obtained could be intelligently and scripturally met.

Repentance may be called initial consecration, but it is no more complete consecration than the alphabet is the complete English language, or any more than New York City is the United States. The alphabet is a part of the English language, and New York City is a part of the United States; likewise repentance is a part of consecration, or consecration begun, but it is not the whole. There may be some immigrants who come to this country, on arriving in New York City think that they have seen the United States (in fact some New Yorkers themselves think that New York City is the bigger part of the United States, judging from their assumed attitude of superiority), that is because they have never seen the thousands of miles of prairies and forest that lie beyond the skyline of Manhattan. So the sinner repenting of his sins does not realize the heights and depths and breadths of stewardship and responsibility that are going to call for a deeper and more complete yielding than he was at first able to make. Sinners may repent, but Christians are commanded to yield themselves unto God, *as those that are alive from the dead*. When a sinner seeks God, he has as his idea a change of relation, but when a believer seeks sanctification he has as his purpose a change of condition.

This consecration on the part of a believer must not only be complete in its substance, but must be for time and eternity. If the consecration is properly and scripturally made, there is no need for a reconsecration. Consecration being a definite transaction and made once for all, does not need to be repeated unless that which has been put upon the altar in consecration has been withdrawn; in which case we have broken our vows with God, and do not need to reconsecrate, but need to repent.

Let the reader remember this is an *experience* we seek and not an experiment, and when seeking do not think you can experiment with God's plan. We once heard a minister say, during a campmeeting service, "Come on friends and try this blessing; if you don't like it the devil will take you back any time." This may have been a very witty and amusing saying on the part of the evangelist, but would never result in anyone's receiving the experience. It is impossible to make the consecration that will please God on any other basis than that it shall be without any mental reservation of ever withdrawing your offering. A scriptural consecration as a condition to being sanctified is a yielding all to God. What about that time that you gave to God and are now spending for your own personal pleasure and profit? What about that money that you consecrated to God and now you are refusing to let Him have it? A little sentimental emotion watered by a few crocodile tears is one thing, while an entire and eternal consecration is another. Reader, have you made a consecration of you and yours to God since you were saved? If God asks for that boy for a preacher, or that girl for a missionary, or that money to build a church, are you consecrated as much as when you sing:

"Here I give my all to thee"?

Consecration is not sanctification in the sense of an operation of the divine Spirit upon the soul, cleansing us from all sin, for consecration is purely the human side of the matter. It is entirely volitional and comes within the limits of man's free moral agency. Man does the consecrating (that is the yielding and submitting); God does the sanctifying or cleansing. Consecration is the human condition for the reception of the blessing. "Do you forsake your sins and surrender?" This is the question asked of every sinner. But the vital question asked of every seeker after

sanctification is, "Is your all on the altar? is your consecration made?" The poet expresses it,
"Is your all on the altar of sacrifice laid,
    Your heart does the Spirit control;
You can only be blest, and have peace and sweet rest,
    As you yield him your body and soul."

The altar seems to be the appointed place where God has been pleased to meet His people in all ages. From the days of righteous Abel unto the present day it has been the place where sacrifices were offered unto God. The altar seems not to have been merely an incident or accident in the matter of carrying out the ritual of the Levitical law, for long before the Levitical law was given there is on record the erection of altars and the offering of sacrifices thereon. It also extends into after dispensations as may be seen by the language of the apostle Paul who says, "We have an altar, whereof they have no right to eat which serve the tabernacle." It also appears quite clear from Ex. 29:37; Matt. 23:19, and others that whatever was put upon the altar was made holy.

Says Professor Dougan Clarke, Professor of Systematic Theology, at Earlham College, after quoting 2 Peter 2:5, "Precisely, if we are priests, we must perform the functions of a priest, and one of these functions is the offering of sacrifice. What, then, are the sacrifices that are to be offered by the Christian priest? Certainly not any expiatory or meritorious sacrifices. These are forever precluded by the fact that Christ hath offered one sacrifice for sins forever. Nothing can be added to and nothing can be sub-

tracted from that infinite and all sufficient offering."
We may add also that the sacrifice of the Christian
is as the apostle puts it, "yielding *ourselves as those
that are alive from the dead.*" "I beseech you therefore, brethren, by the mercies of God, that ye present
your bodies a living sacrifice, holy, acceptable unto
God, which is your reasonable service."

If the reader will follow us now, we will try to lay
down for your consideration what we believe to be a
very clear and simple recipe by which to receive the
blessing of a pure heart. Three things we must consider in the manner of being sanctified; the altar, the
sacrifice, and its purpose. It is quite clear, no doubt,
to the reader that in Old Testament times, under the
plan of Jewish worship, the altar was a very conspicuous quality in their devotion. Before the giving of the Levitical law and the erection of the altar
of the tabernacle it would seem that the altars were
made of earth or unhewn stones (Ex. 20:24, 25). The
description of the altar of the Levitical tabernacle,
which was made of wood overlaid with brass may be
found in Exodus 27:1. These altars, of course, were
erected generally if not always for the purpose of
sacrifice, the sacrificial offering being placed upon
them.

The apostle Paul in his message to the Hebrews
(who no doubt were thoroughly conversant with the
ritualistic worship of the Jews) reminds them that
we, that is, Jews and Gentiles alike, of the New Testament times and plan of worship, "Also have an altar,
whereof they have no right to eat which serve the tab-

ernacle." The old Levitical law is now abolished and
a new order is adopted; in a word, "He taketh away
the first that he may establish the second" (Heb 10:9).
It would seem, therefore, that under the new order of
things Jesus Christ is to become the altar of the
New Testament, as we shall presently see. The con-
trast between the altar of the Old and New Testament
times, therefore is to be found, in that, in the former
it was an altar of material substance, while in the latter
it seems to be a living Christ.

Let us observe next the matter of sacrifices in
Old and New Testament times. In the Old Testament the sacrifices varied from turtle doves, pigeons,
lambs, goats, and up to heifers and bullocks, according
to the ability of the people to give and the object of the
sacrifice that was being made. In the New Testament
no such program was in the mind of God. The sacrifice now must be of another nature and a higher
order. "I beseech you . . . by the mercies of God,"
says the apostle, "that you present your bodies a *living
sacrifice*." Incidentally, this is impossible to the sinner, for he is dead in trespasses and in sins. It would
seem, therefore, that this sacrifice is to be presented by
the Christian (spiritually alive) for the purpose of
proving the *perfect and acceptable will of God*. Having called the reader's attention to the two altars and
the two sacrifices, let us now note the purpose of offering these sacrifices.

After giving a description of the preparation of
the altar to receive the gifts, or sacrifices, that were
to be put upon it, Moses says, "And it shall be an

altar most holy: *whatsoever toucheth the altar shall be holy.*" No doubt the purpose of the offering of such gifts was to make the sacrifice holy. Jesus said to the scribes and Pharisees, "Ye fools, and blind! for whether is greater, the gift, or *the altar that sanctifieth* the gift?" In a word, just as that which was put upon the altar in the Old Testament times was made holy, so the living sacrifice, which is put upon the living altar of the New Testament for the purpose of proving that perfect will of God (this is the will of God even your sanctification), is likewise sanctified or made holy, "for whatsoever toucheth the altar is holy." If there is any doubt in the mind of the reader concerning this matter, let him now turn to the thirteenth chapter of Hebrews and hear again the apostle Paul upon this matter. "We have an altar whereof they have no right to eat which serve the tabernacle." The next verse is a parenthetical verse, calling the reader's attention to the inefficiency of the blood of those beasts to take away sin; while the twelfth verse reminds us of the permanent and final provision and its efficiency to sanctify men by saying, "Wherefore Jesus also, that he might sanctify the people with his own blood, suffered without the gate." That is, that He might do to the living sacrifice of the New Testament exactly what the altar of the Old Testament did to the sacrifice of the Old Testament (that is, make it holy), suffered without the gate. For what was this sacrifice made? *To sanctify the people,* with his own blood. What was the object of placing the sacrifice upon the altar in Old Testament times. "Whatsoever toucheth the altar is holy." What is the object in presenting our bodies a living sacrifice in New Testament times? That we might prove that good and *perfect will of God*. What is the will of God? "This is the will of God, even your sanctification." Wherefore Jesus also, that he might sanctify the people with his own blood, suffered without the gate."

This putting ourselves upon the altar is nothing more than a personal consecration of ourselves, with all our appurtenances, to a personal God. Such a consecration is never urged upon sinners, but as the apostle says, "Yield yourselves unto God *as those that are alive from the dead;*" "a living sacrifice;" for the purpose of being sanctified.

May we ask the reader a plain question? Is your all on the altar? Have you taken an invoice of your consecration; and is all you have, and are given wholly to God in sacrifice, for time and eternity? Do you say it is? Are you telling the truth? Very well, if you are telling the truth, and your all *is* upon the altar, does not God say that whatsoever toucheth the altar is made holy? Does He not give us to understand that the altar sanctifies the gift that is put upon it? You say you have told the truth about being a living sacrifice upon the altar; now does God tell the truth when He declares that whatsoever toucheth the altar is made holy? Very well, then, if you have both told the truth, and the gift is upon the altar, and the altar sanctifies the gift; what can the logical conclusion be, other than that the gift, or sacrifice, is sanctified? But what is the gift? It is *you*, yourself. Then if *you* are the gift upon the altar, *you* are sanctified. If your consecration is rightly and fully made it cannot be otherwise; God's veracity is at stake. My gift is on the altar; the altar sanctifies the gift, *I* am the gift, I am on the altar. *I* am sanctified.

One more step remains and we will be consciously in possession of the experience. It is faith. Everything that we receive in the realms of spiritual or temporal blessing, if it comes from God, must come through the faith channel. Faith is the purchasing medium of God's favor and blessing. When the human condition of sanctification is fully met, so far as consecration is concerned, there remains the indispensable factor of faith, which is necessary to bring to the seeker a full realization that the work is done. After all other conditions have been met, *we must believe*. Whenever all obstructions and impediments have been removed by a perfect complying with God's conditions, there ought to be a spontaneous faith that would reach up and grasp the promise of God.

Let the reader not be deceived and discouraged by those who would (though honestly perhaps, if not wisely) tell you not to take it by faith, but to pray through. There is no way to receive anything from God *except by faith*. You may work yourself into a hysterical frenzy and call the emotional consequence of such act of your own, sanctification; *but you receive nothing from God without faith*. He who disregards this fact closes the door to spiritual benefits to himself. Faith is the substance, it is also the evidence, of things not seen. As to the praying through, this must be done before the reader is on ground to exercise faith. If the writer has a proper conception of what is implied by "praying through," when the last analysis is made, it is nothing more than having complied fully with the provisions of God's promises and met every condition necessary to the reception of God's promised blessing.   Therefore, after we have "prayed through," it is still necessary to exercise a grasping faith if we receive anything from Him.

After all other steps have been taken relative to the obtaining the blessing of a full salvation, there remains the indispensable step of an unswerving faith. "He that cometh to God must *believe* that he is, and that he is a rewarder of them that diligently seek him." But believe what?   The persuasions of your friends, your emotions, your feelings, or your doubts?   No. Believe God's Word.   His Word must always be the basis of your faith.   When conditions have been faithfully and scripturally met, according to the Word of God, the work is done *if you believe* (for without faith it is impossible to please him); not because you feel, not because the folks say you are through, or you are not through; but because *God says*. It is so not because I feel, but because *God says*.   Your lack of faith at this vital point may have deprived you of the much coveted feeling; for the result of the fact cannot take place until the fact itself has occurred; while the fact has been hindered in coming to pass because you have refused to *believe*.

The act of consecration is an experimental fact, you *can know* when it is accomplished.   When this point is reached it becomes our duty and privilege to believe. Believe what? Believe what God says, "Whatsoever toucheth the altar is holy." "The altar sanctifieth the gift." But why believe it? Because I have complied with God's condition, and God says it is so.   That is, God said if I would do certain things, He would do certain things; I have fulfilled my end of the contract, and the fact that I have received is based upon the immutability of His Word. You can depend upon God's Word. It is creative in its nature. When God wanted light He did not have to make a dynamo and string the world with wires; He simply said, "Let there be light *and there was light.*" His word brought it to pass. When God says that whatsoever is put upon the altar of sacrifice, in consecration, is sanctified or made holy, it is so; it is so because He says so, His Word makes it so. It is so to Him the moment the conditions are met; it becomes so to you as soon as you believe, for according to your faith so be it unto you.

If the reader is conscious of having made a complete consecration, without any mental reservation, for time and eternity, he need not go another moment without the experience of entire sanctification; you may have it here and *now.* But how? By simply trusting the blood of Jesus Christ, His Son, to cleanse you from *all* sin; by trusting the altar to sanctify the gift, as God has promised it shall.   Even while reading these lines, will you not lift your heart to God, dear reader, and let your faith take hold of His promise and appropriate this blessing as *yours now?* Now that faith declares the work is done, praise Him and thank

Him for what has happened; for according to your
faith so be it unto you. Let your faith not rest upon
your feelings, but upon "I the Lord have spoken it,
and will do it."

Many have a weakness in their faith because
they want to feel before they believe. This of course
is the wrong order. How foolish to expect the fruits
of faith before you have faith itself. One might as
well expect to quench his thirst before he takes a
drink, or to satisfy his appetite before he eats, as to
have the assurance of sanctification before he has
complied with the conditions upon which it can be
received. "What can be more palpably inconsistent,"
says Rev. Jesse T. Peck, D. D., "than for a man to
say with his lips 'Create in me a clean heart, O God!'
and then in his heart say, 'I do not believe Thou canst
do it; sanctify me wholly, but I do not believe it is His
will for me to be sanctified; cleanse thou me from secret faults, but I expect no such thing to occur; give
me the mind that was in Christ, but such a thing is impossible. And is this not a true representation of much
of the praying which is done in the church for entire
sanctification?"

In answer to the question, "What degree of faith
is necessary to obtain entire sanctification?" Rev.
J. A. Wood says, "No degree. Faith is necessary.
Sanctification is by faith. Believe on the Lord Jesus
Christ and thou shalt be saved. Sanctification re-
quires no greater degree of faith than justification.
Faith in the two instances does not necessarily differ
in *degree,* but in the object for which it is exercised."

As the great Panama Canal opens the way for the union of the two great oceans, so faith opens the way for the union of the human and the divine.

There are three steps in faith, knowledge, assent, and reliance. We must first have a knowledge of the truth; we must then give intellectual assent to the truth, and finally we must depend upon or act accordingly. The real difficult problem of faith is the matter of acting upon the basis of what we know and believe. Faith does not become active, by saying "I believe." But it brings things to pass only in the degree that we act upon the basis of what we say we believe. I believe if I make a certain investment it will make me considerable money, it is safe and sure and the dividends are large; but I make no money. Why? Because while I believed in the investment and had confidence in it, I put no money into it. In other words, I did not act upon the basis of my confidence or faith in the project. I believe if I buy a ticket from the Pennsylvania Railroad Co., they will take me to New York. I know they have the road and the rolling stock, and the efficient trainmen. I even go so far as to buy my ticket; but an hour after the train is gone a friend of mine finds me in the depot. Why have I not gone? Because I didn't get on the train. We must act upon the basis of our faith or we receive no benefits of it. It is not enough for me to believe that Jesus suffered without the gate to sanctify the people with His own blood; or that He prayed for my sanctification. I must meet His conditions, and step out upon His promise, count the work done and act accordingly.

Many can sing, "I can, I will," but they fall down on the *do*. In order to prove a conditional promise, it is always necessary to meet the conditions of the promise. If God says, "Give and it shall be given," then before I can ever expect to receive, I must first learn the value of giving. If He says, "If ye love me, keep my commandments; and I will send you another Comforter," then before we can expect to receive the other Comforter, we must first love Him and keep His commandments. In fact, no conditional promise is to be fulfilled in our lives until we swing clear of ourselves, our surroundings and circumstances, our feelings and emotions, and take God at His word, and govern ourselves accordingly. May both reader and writer have that faith that, "doubts not in our hearts," and thus be able to appropriate the promises of God as belonging to us.

CHAPTER XI

A HUMAN BEING

"The Bible is the only standard of doctrine," says Rev. Jesse T. Peck, D. D. "No schism can be truly grounded in it. Let us cease from ourselves and go to the fountain. In this way only can we see eye to eye and save the church from hazardous speculations and experiments. Opinions above holiness are just as dangerous, and as inevitably false as opinions below it. Innovations which claim to be free from humanity and its frailties, its liabilities to error, and its exposure to sin, are as perilous to the souls of men as those which would reconcile the claims of God and the provision of the gospel with wilful transgression. God's Word gives not the slightest countenance to either, though some teachers may." This quotation of Dr. Peck's is indeed a fitting preface to the subject matter of this chapter.

It is not our purpose to treat this phase of the subject in an exhaustive manner, or to attempt a hairsplitting theological discussion upon technical points; but we are convinced many have become confused in the Christian life and discouraged as often by placing the standard too high as by failing to place it high enough. There is as much danger in placing the standard where it is not, one way as the other. We have often noticed that Bible commentators and exegetes frequently deal extensively in their explanation of scriptures that are already plain, and then when it comes to a difficult passage, where help is most needed, their comments are of such brevity as to be of little value. It also happens that conflicting statements will be the result of Bible interpretation if it is not interpreted in a general sense; that is, no scripture is of private interpretation and scripture must be compared with scripture, so that when the Bible is properly interpreted it never contradicts itself.

It is not likely that we will be able to settle all technical questions relative to holiness, to the satisfaction of everybody; but we do purpose to try to lift the reader out of a maze of seeming contradictions, and fog of confusion, into the golden sunlight of a clear discrimination of just what our privileges, and possibilities may be in the realms of grace.

Let the reader keep in mind, first of all, the fact that holiness never implies anything, more nor less, than the deliverance from all sin. Sanctification has to do with the carnal nature and not the human nature. A sanctified man is not carnal; but he is a human. We expect the carnal to assert itself as long as men are not delivered from its presence; we could expect nothing less of the human. So long as men are carnal, carnality will manifest itself; so long as men are human, human weakness and frailty will manifest themselves. Sanctification removes the carnal nature and gives a pure heart; the sanctified man, therefore, cleansed from all sin we believe should be delivered from the struggling conflict of the carnal nature. But inasmuch as we are not delivered from human frailties and infirmities through sanctification, but rather by a later epochal crisis in the redemptive plan, namely the resurrection, we can expect nothing more than to have to meet the problems of human weakness until the glorious day of our resurrection or glorification, just as we had the problems of the carnal mind until we were sanctified. As a writer of much experience well says, "If the experience of holiness were stripped of the human element, it would be the simplest thing in the world, but, owing to the presence of this complex element of the human nature mixed with the divine, the experience of holiness at times becomes exceedingly complex." We will endeavor to make a clear distinction between the carnal and the human nature, so that we may be able to discriminate between Christian holiness and infallibility.

Perhaps some teachers, in their effort to be uncompromising have been unwise in putting the standard where it is not; but on the other hand no doubt many have been entirely too lax, and have failed to lift the standard to its proper place, as revealed upon the pages of the Sacred Book. There is no place nor provision made, in the life of a normal post-pentecost Christian, for sin, except its complete eradication and extermination. God makes no apology for sin, and no provision for it in the lives of His faithful followers. But "He knoweth our frame and remembereth that we are dust." We must therefore be measured according to our human limitations. God is infinite and infallible; man is finite and fallible. This is surely not lowering the standard of holiness to declare it. No safe and sane teacher of sanctification indicates that such experience confers upon us infallibility.

Let us observe a few of the human elements with which man must reckon, regardless of whatever degree of grace he may possess. First, and we believe fundamental, is the fact that man is always a free moral agent; he always has been, and always will be. God never takes away from man this original quality of volition; in fact, He removes nothing from man by grace that He gave him in creation. We have sometimes heard it said as an objection to sanctification, that an experience where it was impossible to sin was too high for human beings. To this we agree, for we do not believe that any degree of grace takes away our possibility to sin; we shall always be free moral agents, which in itself shows that any man may sin, that any man can sin, but proves as conclusively that no man *must* sin. We have never known any reputable teacher to teach the impossibility of sinning on the part of any human being, regardless of the degree of grace he may possess. Free moral agency has been the inherent right of man since the creation of Adam; God does not destroy this in sanctification; man still has the power to choose his conduct as *he wills to do*. The power to choose, the right to obey or disobey, is the moral privilege of the sanctified man as well as the justified, or even the sinner. Holiness neither destroying nor rendering inactive this volitional quality in human nature, the sanctified man finds himself involved constantly with the making of moral choice, which at any time could be made wrong if he so willed. May the reader never be led into this error that a sanctified man *cannot* sin.

The fact that we are human and fallible, also makes us susceptible to temptation. Jesus Christ was both human and divine, and therefore susceptible to temptation. God cannot be tempted, neither tempteth He any man; yet we are told that Jesus was tempted in all points like as we, yet, without sin. Why was He tempted *like as we?* Because *like as we* he was human, having taken upon himself the human nature, which was susceptible to temptation. It was for this reason that the apostle declared, "I keep under my body, and bring it into subjection: lest that by any means, when I have preached to others, I myself should be a castaway" (1 Cor. 9:27). The sanctified man has all the human elements with which to reckon; appetities, passions, human propensities and human desires must all be kept in their proper and lawful relation, in a word, the body with all its natural desires must be brought into subjection; and though we may be tempted and tried we can be overcomers in the warfare of grace because, "greater is he that is in you, than he that is in the world."

The human element in the holy man or woman which can be tempted is the same that was in Adam when he was tempted in Eden. Carnality is hell's greatest ally, and the cleansed and sanctified man is free from it, thank God! However, he is a free moral agent and susceptible to being tempted. There may be a clamor of the world without and the physical weakness of the human from within, with which to contend, but like the apostle, we can keep our bodies in subjection. "He that ruleth his own spirit is greater than he that taketh a city." Alexander could not only take a city, but empires, but died in debauchery, a young man, because he could not control his own body. Oh, for men and women with clean hands and pure hearts, who can master themselves.

Let us not lower the standard of New Testament Christian integrity on the one hand, nor hold it above that which is scriptural on the other; but may we seek to know the truth, regardless of whether man is humiliated or exalted. Says one writer upon the subject of Christian holiness, "To pray for deliverance from those things which are occasioned by the body is, in effect, to pray for deliverance from the body." To pray for deliverance from that which is the natural consequence of being physical and human is to pray for impossibilities and absurdities, praying that God would break into and destroy the inexorable program of natural law, by allowing us to continue in the body, and yet delivering us from all the natural and lawful consequences that accompany such union. "One might as well pray," as some writer has declared, "to be angels and men at the same time, or mortal and immortal at the same time." God always answers the prayer of faith for the deliverance from sin; but so far as physical and human frailties are concerned; we are often and most generally given fortitude and grace with which to bear them, as in the case of the apostle Paul, who besought the Lord thrice to deliver him, but whose only answer was, "My grace is sufficient for thee," to which the apostle responded with Christian fortitude and courage that was undaunted, and said, "Most gladly therefore will I glory in mine *infirmities* [not sins] that the power of Christ may rest upon me."

In discussing the problems of the physical man, we cannot overlook his nervous system. It is a part of physical man, and it is not carnal to possess nerves, whether good or bad. This faculty of the physical or human being is, therefore, a factor with which we are called to reckon until the redemption of the body, to wit, the resurrection. So much has been said in ridicule about nervous spells among holiness people that to mention such a matter is to raise the question in the minds of many as to whether or not one is not trying to erect a subterfuge for the old man, and apologize for the manifestations of the carnal nature. We realize that two mistakes have been made in regard to this matter, both of which have been decidedly hurtful. First, that of confusing nervousness and carnality. Second, that of excusing carnality under the guise of nervousness. We cannot afford to dodge an earnest effort to know the truth in this matter because some have made these blunders. To accuse a person who is a nervous wreck and extremely nervous and sensitive of being carnal and hypocritical is often an unfair, a harsh and un-Christian accusation. To excuse the manifestations, on the other hand, of carnality under the false pretense that it was a nervous condition, and allow the subject to go on in self satisfaction, deceived, and with a false profession of holiness, will in the end prove to be an irremediable blunder. An abnormal and diseased nervous system is no more carnality than is the measles or the small pox or any other physical deformity, and the manifestation of such disorder is no more a manifestation of carnality than would be the holding your hand to your face when you have the toothache.

Physical infirmities are purely human and physical and are perfectly compatible with a holy heart and pure love. They are the product of our human or physical nature. Sin is a moral defilement and has its source in our moral, and not our physical being. Infirmities may sometimes embarrass and humiliate, but do not produce that condemnation which characterizes the guilt of a disobedient child of God. Sin is wilful and against light and knowledge and against God, and always produces that condemnation which disqualifies you as a Christian (Rom. 8:1). Infirmities and human weaknesses result from our fallibility, and not from our carnal or depraved nature; but sin has its source in a moral perverseness that is wilful and intentionally wicked. We believe we have given a clear, logical and scriptural distinction between the human and the carnal on this point of "nervousness vs. depravity." That God does deliver from every wicked purpose and intention by His sanctifying grace is clearly stated in the Scriptures, that blunders and mistakes,

Scriptures on Sanctification
Ephesians 5:25,27.
1 Thess. 4,:3+4
1 Cor 1:30.
John 17:17
1 Thess. 5:43
Hebrews 12:14.

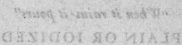

which are the product of our human or physical man, will continue to be a problem as long as we are physical and human is equally as clearly stated. As long as we are human, we are susceptible to human weakness; we will have human problems, and the deficiencies of fallible creatures with which to contend. Physical appetites and desires are natural and normal to a human, and lawful and legitimate in themselves; *they are not an evidence of depravity,* and the scriptural injunction concerning them is that they shall be brought into subjection and controlled in their lawful and legitimate channels, that sin may not reign in *these mortal bodies.* Lawful and temperate must be the unrelenting program concerning the human nature and its capacities; but crucifixion and destruction is the program concerning the carnal nature and its capacities.

A sanctified man is no less sanctified because he is human. Jesus himself is an outstanding example of this fact. He became tired, hungry, thirsty, weak, indignant and severe. It was Jesus who, weary and tired, fell asleep in the ship in the midst of a storm. It was Jesus who asked the woman at the well for a drink; it was Jesus who fasted forty days and was afterward an hungered; it was Jesus who under a sense of righteous indignation, "looked upon the Pharisees, with anger and was grieved with the hardness of their hearts." It was Jesus who pronounced woe in no unmistakable manner upon the hypocrites in His day; it was Jesus who suffered in the garden and on the cross, mentally and physically; yet all of these weaknesses do not discredit Him morally nor spiritually, nor put a question mark behind His divinity, nor make Him any less the Savior of the world, or the Son of God. In like manner these human and physical weaknesses make you no less a sanctified soul; it is only yielding to the demand of these things unlawfully that can bring upon us God's frown of disapproval.

The body or physical man is like a crying baby; it has its wants, but like the baby is dependent upon the parent to gratify these; so the body is dependent upon the soul, which gives direction to the organs of the body, to gratify its desires. These old bodies cannot sin, in and of themselves; they have no more power to sin than the clothes that are on them; but like an indulgent child the passions, appetites and propensities that are human may cause considerable annoyance, unless properly disciplined and brought under control. This position is sustained by the Revised Version of 1 Cor. 9:27, which says, "But I buffet my body and bring it into bondage." W. B. Godbey, noted Greek scholar says, "I keep under my body and subjugate it." The Pulpit Commentary, edited by Spence and Excell, and published by Funk and Wagnalls, in its comment upon this passage says, "Literally, I bruise my body, and lead it about as a slave." At any rate it may be seen that the New Testament standard is not a deliverance from the problems of the physical man, but that he shall be disciplined, and perhaps at times rigidly disciplined, which is not always a pleasant task to say the least.

It would be well before we conclude this part of our subject not to overlook the fact that the power of thought is also a factor with which we shall always be called to reckon. Like that of volition or free moral agency, it is never destroyed by any degree of grace, and is often the power behind the throne, for it is the foundation of all our actions. One of the greatest influences in creating in us a course of conduct, either good or bad, is that of thought or imagination. Action is usually stimulated by thinking. Some people seem to think that so long as they do not sin in word or deed, their thoughts may be permitted to run rampant. We are careful of our words, we control our actions, we discipline our feelings and govern our conduct, but allow our thought to run lawless and unrestrained anywhere upon any subject. There is no limit to its range, no place too sacred for its entrance, no associations too vile for its companionship. Like the invisible spirits that fill the air, it flits unseen among angels and devils, and sips as it will, at fountains good and evil. It dominates the sensitive nature, and often shows itself to be a regular anarchist when effort is made to bring it into the realm of governmental jurisdiction. It often makes hypocrites of us, and robs us of many good opportunities, by living and acting a lie. As for example, we are in the house of God, our eyes are upon the preacher, our ears appear to be at attention and we sit there, apparently in the attitude of a true worshipper; but all the time our thoughts have carried us away to the golf course, or to the movies, or perhaps we are down at the office, at least we are losing the good of the truth we should be receiving because we have not brought our thinking into subjection. May we not well ask in the language of one writer, who well says, "What avails then if the sanctified exterior, and even the outward practices of our life seem to conform to the law of God, if the imagination is allowed to run rampant in forbidden fields of thought." A foul imagination is death to vital Christianity, they cannot live and thrive in the same temple. Action good or bad is always preceded by thought relative to that action. No man ever goes into forbidden paths whose thought did not precede him there. Holiness can never be maintained without a bringing of this faculty of our being into subjection, disciplining it, and making it to stay in its lawful and rightful channels.

Rev. Asbury Lowery, D. D., says, "Much of the gross vice which reeks in our cities and breathes its malaria over the whole land, is generated and hatched in the ovarium of illicit thought. If the bodies of men were transparent, and the brooding of meditation were an object of vision, what a nest of unclean things the mind would reveal." The thoughts are being used to give birth to actions that are entirely out of harmony with holiness of heart and life.

There is an element of moral fallibility in all professors of holiness for no rational person claims infallibility. The great grace of sanctification by its powerful and instantaneous work will cleanse us from all sin, and will rectify the will, poise the passions, hold

in check all innocent, and eradicate all unholy appetites and enthrone that holiness, without which no man
shall see the Lord, upon the citadel of the soul; thus
cleansing him from all sin and making him master of
himself. Blessed is the man who has been redeemed
from sin, and who has brought his body into subjection
and mastered the problems of the human or physical
man so that he can testify to the possession of clean
hands and a pure heart.

CHAPTER XII

WHY?

This is an inquisitive age, men are not only asking the what, the how, and the where of certain problems, but are equally and as vitally concerned about the why of the matter. We have endeavored to show to the reader in the preceding chapters the what, and the how, and the where of sanctification; we now offer for your consideration two or three important reasons as to why we should be sanctified.

The first, and we believe a very important reason, is because it is God's will (1 Thes. 4:3). We are not advocating this doctrine because it is sponsored by any particular wing of ecclesiastical officialdom, or because the intellectuals are either for or against it, but because it is the will of God. How can any person be deceived into believing that God is pleased with him, when he is deliberately disregarding His will in this matter. There are other things, also that are the will of God, to be sure, but these do not preclude the importance of the matter of sanctification. The will of the father ought to always be the delight of every obedient child; and the child who knows his father's will and does not conform to it is surely a disobedient and ungrateful child.

If the will of God concerning me is that I should be sanctified, as a child of God I certainly should be submissive to His will and obedient to His wishes pertaining to my best and highest good. Obedience is the keynote to fidelity. If I am to remain in a justified relation to my heavenly Father, I must be obedient to His will; not to do so is to bring condemnation upon my own soul, and to put a question mark in the minds of all that know me concerning my sincerity. The condition of fellowship with God and each other as Christian people is that we walk in the light. If I know it is God's will for me to be sanctified, that Jesus suffered without the gate to sanctify me with His own blood, and I remain coldly indifferent to so great and costly a provision of the divine will concerning me, how can I longer be disobedient in this matter and keep His favor upon me? If it is God's will, it should be the will of all His obedient children.

Second, if it is the will of God, our keeping saved is contingent upon our being sanctified; for no person can retain the favor of God upon himself and at the same time resist God's desire, or refuse to submit to His will. It is not only a matter of keeping saved, from a standpoint of obedience to God, however, that is involved; but the experience itself has a preserving or keeping quality in it, and it would seem from many scriptures that it is a great preventative for backsliding. Let the reader turn to such scriptures as 1 Thes. 5:23; Jude 1; Rom. 5:12, and others and he will at once be impressed with this fact.

After almost every revival the common complaint is that the converts do not stick. Many who made bright professions disappear from the ranks of God. Just what percentage of backsliding follows our evangelistic work, it would be hard to tell; but it is sufficiently large to cause all sincere and earnest people to seek a remedy. Where can such remedy be found? We believe it could be largely found in our going on unto perfection, or getting sanctified. Hear the exhortation of the apostle (Heb. 6:1), "Therefore leaving the principles of the doctrine of Christ let us go on unto perfection; *not laying again the foundation of repentance.* What else can this mean, other than to go on unto perfection is the preventative for going back again to repentance? Laying again the foundation, indicates that they have gone back again to the starting place, and he is urging them on to perfection to prevent this. Surely if we do not obey God in regard to this matter we are disobeying Him just as much as if we disregarded His commandments relative to any other matter. How much disobedience may we indulge in and remain justified?

If salvation from all sin is provided for us and required of us, then no man coming to a knowledge of that fact can be fully justified who does not seek it and live in possession of it. This is a crisis in Christian experience, and many we fear have already forfeited their vital communion with God and fellowship with the saints because they have refused to walk in the light and face their obligation concerning this matter. Dr. Lowery asks, "Can such a person have any living hope of heaven? What is the difference in the rejection of pardon and the rejection of sanctification?"

We are inclined to think the latter is the worse of the two (Heb. 10:28).

If the reader will turn to the twelfth of Hebrews and read the fourteenth and fifteenth verses he will see that the apostle is exhorting us to follow peace with all men and, "the sanctification, without which no man shall see the Lord" (R. V.). But wait a moment! When we read into the next verse he tells us why He wants us to heed this exhortation. Not alone that you shall see God; but, "lest any man fail of the grace of God," or as the marginal reading has it "lest any man *fall from the grace of God.*" Here then is a plain statement to the effect that following after holiness is the preventative from falling from the grace of God.

The apostle seems to indicate this also when he prays, "The very God of peace sanctify you wholly, and I pray God your whole spirit, soul and body *be preserved* [that is, kept] blameless unto the coming of the Lord Jesus Christ." Oh, for a keeping grace that will establish and solidify the people of God. We need it. We need it badly. Something that will conserve the work of justification and regeneraton.

It is every Christian's business to keep out from under condemnation, for, "There is . . . no condemnation to them that are in Christ Jesus." They that are justified by faith have peace with God. We must not lose sight of the fact that this justification is retained only upon one condition, that is obedience. Disobedience and justification are incompatible terms. "Minding God" must be the business of every true disciple of our Lord. To disobey is to forfeit our justified relation. If I am to keep saved I must obey; when light is given I must walk in it; when I know the truth I must obey it. If the reader is a child of God, may we not ask, "Does it mean nothing to you, that He has called you unto holiness? Is it of no vital importance to you, that the matter has been positively declared to be the will of God? Have you no obligation, as a Christian, concerning any of these exhortations or commands relative to sanctification? Can you know that this is the will of God concerning you; that without it no man shall see the Lord; that Jesus suffered outside the gate to provide it for you, and be utterly indifferent to it all, and have the consciousness that God is pleased with you? Is it any worse for a sinner to deliberately refuse pardon, than it is for a believer to deliberately refuse to go on to perfection, or be sanctified? Does not the sinner forfeit the approbation of God by his disobedience; shall we expect the believer to be less guilty than he? If God wills that you be sanctified, and your will is to the contrary, are you and He agreed? "How can two walk together except they be agreed?" The question that confronts every child of God should not be, "Can I get to heaven without holiness?" for the Bible has made that very plain; but the question should be, "How long can I refuse to made holy, and remain justified?" One well known writer upon this subject says, "I am fully convinced that a neglect on the part of regenerated souls to seek entire sanctification, is a more fruitful occasion of losing the witness of justification, and of backsliding, than all other sources combined. Indeed, it includes virtually all other causes." Quoting the writer further he says, "Who that believes in the possibility of temporary or final apostasy could suggest a mode of backsliding more effectual than to allow the sinful propensities of our nature to remain undisturbed; to disobey the great law of progress which is revealed as sacredly binding upon every converted man; to neglect the blood which offers to cleanse from all unrighteousness, and decline as a thing of naught the purifying baptism of the Holy Ghost?"

The third reason for seeking the experience of sanctification, is to be found in the fact that it is the great source of spiritual power that will enable us to execute a faithful, consistent and useful stewardship (Acts 1:8). It is the paramount need for successful service. The Son of God knew the importance of this matter, consequently when he sent His disciples out He commanded them to tarry at Jerusalem until they received the promise of the Father.

That the Church is in great need of something that will make it more spiritual, more aggressive and more successful, is the opinion of most spiritual people. Many professing Christians are notorious for their barren and fruitless lives; many are making excuses instead of making good. If souls are not saved, whatever other designs are accomplished, the ultimate purpose of our stewardship is defeated. Organization, education, musical talent, fine buildings and a cultured ministry can never atone for the absence of the Holy

Spirit's power, which is the promised inheritance and privilege of the Church. Oh, how the present day Church needs the promised power, through the baptism of the Holy Spirit, in sanctifying efficacy!

At the ascension of Jesus, the Church numbered about one hundred and twenty. This represents the fruits of the three years' ministry before Pentecost. But under the baptism of the Holy Spirit in pentecostal fullness, three thousand were converted in a single day. They had something more than social standing, wealth and scholarship, in fact they had none of these; but they had the Holy Spirit in His fullness; they had received the promise of the Father and had that power they were promised when the Holy Spirit came.

What minister without this second crisis in his experience, this pentecostal baptism that gives power, has not felt his lack and weakness and been forced often to acknowledge defeat because of a lack of spiritual power in his message? Says Rev. A. M. Hills, D. D., "I have seen a beloved ministerial brother with an admiring congregation at his feet, with a salary of $5,000 a year and many generous gifts from loving friends besides, with an influence and position that most men might covet, come home from a Sabbath day of preaching, and cover his face with his hands, and mourn over the apparent fruitlessness of his work, and declare that he had missed his calling. I looked at the brother with all the pity of a sympathetic heart. I did not know then what was the trouble with the gifted man that had a place and opportunity that an angel might have coveted. I know now. The baptism of the Holy Ghost would have increased his usefulness fourfold, and made his task a perpetual joy, and filled his heart with gladness like that of heaven. He had culture, he had talent, he had wit, he had genius, everything but the anointing of the Holy Ghost, without which he was poor indeed." Would the reader have that power, that courage, that fruitfulness and success that is the desire of every true child of God; then tarry until ye be endued with power from on high.

The fourth reason that we offer the reader for being sanctified is, that it is an indispensable necessity for citizenship in heaven. It is the quality of moral and spiritual integrity that will be demanded of us for entrance there. The editor of the Christian Witness says, "There are many reasons that inspire us with a desire for heaven. Some want to go because they want to escape the pains of hell; others want to go because they want to meet their loved ones that have gone on before; others because they want to get rid of those things which in this life are disagreeable and hard; others would like to go because it is a place of enjoyment and rejoicing; all these are improper. Heaven will be all of these and will have all these inducements fulfilled, but there is a motive higher than these that inspires some. It is that they may be better acquainted with our wonderful God and His wonderful Son. They want to be holy that they may dwell with Him forever and enjoy His fellowship."

He who cannot see in the nature of God an imperative demand for holiness as a requisite of fitness for heaven has never had a real vision of Him. A vision of God always makes a man see his need, just as it did the prophet Isaiah (Isa. 61:1, 7). As Dean Alford once put it, "Because God is holy, essentially, absolutely, unchangeably and transcendently holy; therefore He infinitely loves holiness and infinitely hates sin. He delights only in that which possesses His own nature and bears His image. He is the infinite model and source of holiness and desires that all His creatures should be holy, because it is written, *"Be ye holy for I am holy."*

Would the reader be convinced of this truth, let him read a few such statements of Holy Writ as, Psa. 24:3, 4; Heb. 12:14; Matt. 5:8; Rev. 21:27. If he would know something of his personal obligation concerning the matter let him read, 2 Pet. 2:21; Jude 5; Heb. 10:28, 29; 1 Cor. 3:16, 17, and others. If he would know whether or not such quality is obtainable, let him read 1 Thes. 4:7, 8; 2 Cor. 9:8; 1 Thes. 2:10; 1 Pet. 1:22; Heb. 13:12; and many more that are equally as clear upon this matter. Knowing the standard that is required to ultimate salvation, and knowing that such standard is possible, and knowing the consequence if we fail to obtain it, how can we do less than say, "Holiness is imperative, holiness is possible"?

When we say that holiness is the standard for entrance into heaven, we are invariably confronted with the question, "What is to become of all the good people who died in the triumphs of Christian faith?" Let the reader not be so much concerned about those who died in the triumphs of faith, for we can well assure him that they never went to hell. Hell is not made for justified souls. Every person who dies justified, will be cleansed through the merits of the vicarious sacrifice of Jesus Christ. But do not overlook the fact that in order to have the cleansing benefits of the atonement we must "Walk in the light as he is in the light." We cannot dodge the truth and refuse to face our moral obligation in regard to holiness and be indifferent to the provision God has made for us and continue justified. Jesus said on one occasion, "Except ye be converted, and become as little children, ye shall not enter into the kingdom of heaven." We take it therefore that conversion puts us in the same relation to God (morally) as the little child. The apostle Paul says, "As by the offense of one, judgment came upon all men to condemnation; even so by the righteousness of one, the free gift came upon all men unto justification of life." It would appear from this statement that the entire human family became condemned in Adam, but were all justified (not regenerated) in Christ. Now this child that is justified through the meritorious sacrifice of Jesus is saved, up to the time and place of moral responsibility. When this child reaches the years of accountabilty, it is now confronted wih the scriptural injunction, "Ye must be born again." Now with the coming of this light there comes also responsibility. The child has now reached the age of moral decision, it must either obey the demand to be regenerated, born again, or it must forfeit its infantile justification (which was only a merciful provision made by a good God to carry it safely through childhood,) "Except ye become as little children." How are little children? They are without light or moral responsibility. When the child comes to a knowledge of its duty it must obey and walk in the light, or the blood no longer cleanses.

Now, as we have already stated, the converted man and the child occupy the same (morally responsible) relation to God. Just as the child when it comes to the years of accountability must obey the scriptural injunction, "Ye must be born again," or forfeit its justified relation to God, so the justified man when he comes to the place of light and responsibility concerning sanctification must walk in the light or forfeit his justification and like the little child automatically become a sinner. Justification can never be upon any other basis than that of obedience. If we walk in the light the blood cleanses; if we do not the light that we have becomes darkness, and how great is that darkness. Others may die in the triumphs of Christian faith knowing nothing of sanctification, but if they did it was because they walked in the light they had. If their attention had been brought to this matter, and their responsibility had been seen concerning it, and they had deliberately neglected and disregarded it, they would never have died in a victorious faith. We might add that the reader perhaps has had much light upon this matter, and has been made to feel his obligation, but has dodged it up to this good hour; let me exhort you dear soul, walk in the light and the blood of Jesus Christ his Son will cleanse you from all sin. If we refuse the light it will become darkness; "If therefore the light that is in thee be darkness, how great is that darkness!" (Matt. 6:23).

Commenting upon this matter the Rev. Jesse T. Peck, D. D., says, "There hence arises a strong probability that many reach the state of entire sanctification without the knowledge of others. This fact may exist without evidence to us of its existence. For the want of well defined views, or a precise style of faith that secures the witness to that special work, it may not be known (as entire sanctification) even to themselves. This fact may exist without evidence of its existence to us. In such the completion of the work being known to God would be sufficient. . . . The conclusion of the whole matter then must be this: God will permit nothing unholy to enter heaven; He has not two sets of conditions for believers. All the saved are entirely cleansed from sin in this life through faith in Christ; the only obscurity in the system being that the time and manner of bringing the conditions into exercise may be, in many instances, concealed from short-sighted and ignorant man."

If, therefore, sanctification is God's will; if it is the great preventative from backsliding; if it is the source of spiritual power and usefulness and the divine requisite for admission to heaven, we certainly can ask the reader no less than to follow peace with all men and holiness, without which no man shall see the Lord (Heb. 12:14).

CHAPTER XIII

THE EVIDENCE

We are approaching now a subject upon which there is a remarkable scarcity of writing; at least considering the important place it occupies in the plan of man's redemption. God purposes to give such sufficient evidence of His works of grace, that no one need to be constantly in an atmosphere of speculation. This evidence is an important factor, and the balance wheel in our spiritual fidelity and progress. Mr. Wesley once said, relative to this matter: "It is necessary to defend and explain this truth, because there is danger on the right hand and on the left. If we deny it, there is danger lest our religion degenerate into formality, lest, having a form of godliness, we neglect, if not deny, the power of it. If we allow it, but do not understand what we allow, we are liable to run into all the wildness of enthusiasm. It is therefore needful in the highest degree to guard those who fear God from both these dangers, by a scriptural and rational illustration and confirmation of this momentous truth."

No person who reads such scriptures as Rom. 8:15, 16; Heb. 10:14, 15, and others of like nature, can deny or doubt the fact of a direct witness of the Spirit to the operations of His grace upon the soul; and with such scriptures as 1 Jno. 5:17, 19; 1 Jno.

166

3:14, and others, it is plainly evident that we may know of the work that God hath wrought in us, beyond the place of mere hypothesis.

It may be well to state at the outset of this chapter that inasmuch as we are writing upon the evidence of sanctification, that so far as the direct witness is concerned, there is no difference in the witness of the Spirit to being born again and that of being sanctified. The manner of the witness is the same, the difference consisting only in the matter, or rather the thing that is being witnessed to. One is the assurance that we have been made a child of God, by being born again (Rom. 8:15, 16), and the other is the assurance of our sanctification (Heb. 10:14, 15); the witness of the Spirit to both works being an inward attestation to the particular thing that has been accomplished.

Before we undertake to give to the reader our conception of the witness of the Spirit; let us first observe what it is not. First, it is not any physical emotion or human demonstration. Whatever the witness is or is not, it is abiding, so long as the work abides the witness also abides. It is not a spasmodic something that we have at certain intervals, when certain outward influences may be playing upon our emotions, and then lose, when we are in the midst of fiery trials. If our emotions constituted the witness, then when our emotions were not stirred we would find ourselves without the witness. The witness would be as fluctuating and undependable as our feelings. As one writer expresses it, "One would know he has religion only when he is excited. Between his religious eruptions he is like an extinct volcano, sometimes the snow and ice of hoary winter lying upon the bald summits of his nature defy the Son of God's mid-summer to melt them away. If such a man's religion never ascends so high as to become a matter of consciousness in his cooler hours, it also never descends so low as to have anything to do with his life. . . . And not only is he not conscious of possessing religion in his cooler hours; but when he is in that state the world does not know it either. He and the world only know he has religion when he is excited, and to tell the truth, the Lord does not know it at all."

There has always been a decided weakness on the part of some to measure their degree of grace by the volume of their noise and demonstration. They become discouraged and despondent if this "high pressure" stuff is not continued day in and day out. They thus make themselves a good target for Satan, who takes advantage of their weakness right here. If they do not act or feel like others who seem to be especially blessed, Satan loses no opportunity to discourage them. He says, "You don't feel like Brother A," or "you don't act like Brother B," or "you haven't got what Brother C says he got when he professed the blessing." All this may be true, so far as feeling or acting as others is concerned, but a deliberate falsehood of Satan so far as your own experience is concerned. The manifestations upon which he is seeking to center your attention are not the evidences of any work of grace (though they may sometimes be the result of the evidence), but are the product of your own peculiar temperament and personality. Thank God, the witness of the Spirit is a more dependable and lasting something, than a mere effervescent exaltation of our physical emotions. These we love to see and we pray God that the emotional in our religion may ever be a vital factor toward encouraging our hearts in the things of God; but beloved, do not mistake the human manifestations of the creature for the divine assurance, which is invisible to the natural eye, but clearly revealed to the intuitions of the soul.

Second, it is not the gift of tongues, nor any other *gift*. While it is a historical fact and so recorded upon the pages of sacred history that upon the day of Pentecost they "began to speak with other tongues," not unknown tongues, this phenomenon which accompanied the outpouring of the Spirit, no one acquainted with the facts will deny, nor will they dispute the fact that on a few occasions afterward there is recorded a repetition of this demonstration at the time of the outpouring of the Spirit. That this remarkable occurrence, however, is not the witness of the Spirit to any degree of grace may be seen from the following reasons: First, nowhere in the Scripture is it ever indicated that this speaking in tongues was the evidence of sanctification, or any other work of grace. Not even on the occasions when it occurred is it suggested that this demonstration was the witness of the Spirit. The mere fact that it is recorded that they did speak with *other* tongues, must never be misconstrued into making that the infallible evidence or the witness of the Spirit.

They heard the sound as of a mighty rushing wind also. Why not make that an evidence of the baptism? There appeared unto them cloven tongues like as of fire and sat upon each of them. Why not make that the evidence of the pentecostal experience or sanctification? Surely we have the same reason for assuming that these are evidences of the pentecostal experience that we have for saying that speaking with tongues is the witness. They all three occurred and none of them is mentioned as the infallible proof of any work of grace. By what manner of interpretation do you select one manifestation from the three and make it the evidence to the exclusion of the others, when you have the same authority for assuming that the sound of the rushing wind and the tongues like as of fire are likewise evidences? Why not say that if we do not hear the sound like a mighty rushing wind we have not the evidence; or if we do not have the tongues like as of fire sit upon each of us we are not sanctified? Certainly we have the same ground for making one the evidence of the work of God as we have for the other. How ridiculous to pick out one of three distinct manifestations and without any authority whatsoever make that the evidence of the pentecostal experience to the exclusion of others equally as manifest and bid with the same authority to be equally recognized.

The apostle asks, "Do all speak with tongues?" The form of this question, as the reader will see if he will turn to the twelfth chapter of First Corinthians, is indicative of a negative answer, and is equivalent to saying, "that all *do not* speak with tongues." Here we are faced with the absurdity, if tongues is the evidence of any degree of grace, of being denied the witness. Are we, therefore, to assume that only certain ones who have the favor of God upon them are to be entitled to the evidence of that fact? Is it not a fact that the office work of the Holy Spirit is to witness to the works of God in redemption? Is it not a further fact that all who possess the works of God's grace in the plan of salvation are entitled to such witness or evidence? If therefore all do not speak with tongues and yet all are entitled to the witness of the Spirit it is plainly evident that this speaking in tongues is not the witness of the Spirit. If the gift of tongues is the evidence of pentecostal salvation, then only those who speak with tongues have pentecostal sanctification, an assertion which is so ridiculously absurd as to be both unreasonable and unscriptural.

If the gift of tongues had been the evidence of any work of grace whatsoever, we could not reconcile it with the fact that the apostle would have spoken so disparagingly about it and even discouraged it. It is not likely that the apostle would have sought to prevent anyone's having the witness of the Spirit, or discouraged it in any manner whatsoever. In 1 Cor. 14:19 he says, "Yet in the church I had rather speak five words with my understanding, that by my voice I might teach others also, than ten thousand words *in an unknown tongue*." Is Paul saying here that he prefers not have the witness of the Spirit or evidence of what God has done for him? Yet this is exactly what he intimates if the speaking with tongues is the evidence of any work of grace. He continues again, "Though I speak with the tongues of men and of angels, and have not charity [love] I am become as sounding brass or a tinkling cymbal." Evidently he does not lay much stress on the matter of speaking with tongues; yet if speaking with tongues was evidence of his acceptance, he would not only have cause to rejoice for the privilege of speaking with tongues, but would glory in the fact that it was the witness of his acceptance with God. If the speaking with tongues was the evidence of pentecostal sanctification he *would* have the love which he says he may not have though speaking either as men or angels. From this language of the apostle there is evidently something of greater importance than speaking with tongues, yet if this is the witness of the Spirit to any degree of grace whatsoever, it is fundamentally important and indispensable.

The condition which existed when Paul wrote this language, is strikingly manifest in this generation. Many there are who can speak with tongues who seem to possess no other Christian virtues at all. The writer is personally acquainted with those who do not manifest the gracious principles of Christianity in their everyday living; though they speak "in tongues." We have known of others whose moral lives were questionable beyond measure, who were untruthful, dishonest, in adultery, yet they spoke with tongues. If the speaking with tongues is the witness of the Spirit to sanctification, or the evidence that we have received our pentecost, then we are facing the moral absurdity of the Holy Ghost giving the witness where it does not belong. Would the Holy Spirit witness a lie? Could a man possess the witness of the Spirit when he refuses to pay his debts, when he is untruthful, or when he is immoral? Why should the Holy Ghost confer upon him the evidence that he has an experience which it is plainly visible, even to short sighted man, that he does not possess?

It is not our purpose here to enter into a discussion of the tongues problem, concerning its merits or demerits; we are only trying to show that the gift of speaking with tongues is not the witness of the Spirit to sanctification, nor incidentally the evidence of any other work of divine grace. If speaking with tongues is the evidence of sanctification, then when Paul says, "Greater is he that prophesieth, than he that speaketh with tongues," does he mean to imply that it would be better to have natural ability than the witness of God's Spirit to our regeneration or sanctification? Perhaps this is the reason that some of our modern preachers are so adept in dodging this matter of the baptism of the Holy Ghost and prefer to have a fruitless ministry year after year, depending upon their own scholastic attainments rather than the help of the Spirit. Does Paul mean to say he would rather be a minister than to have the witness of the Spirit to his own heart, the assurance which he himself has declared that God has promised to all His children (1 Thes. 1:5)? Yet this is precisely what he says if the witness of the Spirit consists of speaking in tongues.

But to put the question beyond further controversy, and that you may not be in doubt, Paul tells you *exactly* the purpose for which tongues were given. Is it for an evidence of an inward work of grace? It is not. Is it the witness or evidence of our relation to God? It is not. Is it the Spirit's testimony to our sanctification? It is not. Speak up, Paul, and tell us the purpose of tongues. Listen! He says, "Wherefore tongues are for a sign, *not to them that believe,* but *to them that believe not.*" It is not a sign, or evidence, to believers, but to them that believe *not.* In a word it has no more to do with the moral transformation of the inward man, than the raising of the widow's son at the gate of Nain. No doubt the object of all of Christ's miracles were for a sign to them that *believed not,* and unquestionably this strange manifestation is for a like purpose. At least that is what the apostle says concerning the matter. Beloved, let us stay in the middle of the road and not wrest the scriptures to our own hurt and the hurt of others. The witness of the Spirit is not for a sign to *others,* or those that believe not; but to those that believe (1 Jno. 5:10). Hence the witness of the Spirit and the gift of tongues are just the opposite in their purpose, and for an entirely different people; one for the believers, and the other for the "believers *not.*" The witness of the Spirit is not something that is visible to the natural eye; but something that produces an inward assurance, that the work to which He witnesses has been accomplished.

We have discussed briefly these two errors relative to the evidence of God's work in our souls, let us examine the matter from a standpoint of what it is.

If it is not the gift of tongues, if it is not physical feeling, or emotion, what is it?

The scriptural witness of the Spirit, or evidence of our sanctification is twofold; it is direct and indirect, that is, it is God's Spirit bearing witness with our spirit. It is an inward assurance wrought by the Spirit of God; giving us an inward consciousness of the work having been accomplished. It is just as profound a conviction that the work has been done as your conviction was before it was done that you needed such a work, and is wrought by the same Holy Spirit. As to the technical nature of this inward revelation; it is rather difficult to analyze, as Jesus once said, "The wind bloweth where it listeth, and thou hearest the sound thereof, but canst not tell whence it cometh, and whither it goeth; so is every one that is born of the Spirit."

Mr. Wesley once said, "It is hard to find words in the language of men to explain the deep things of God; indeed there are none that will adequately express what the children of God experience." The best, therefore that we can say concerning the witness of God's Spirit, is, that it is an inward persuasion, or conviction, by the Spirit that the work is done. Just as the Spirit came and made you feel your need, your sense of lostness and your utter undoneness without Him; now that the work is done, that same Holy Spirit gives you an inward conviction of the fact that the need which He so clearly revealed to you, has been met.

The inward testimony of the Spirit puts the doctrine of assurance out of the realm of doubt. While we know that the believer has in his heart a testimony of the Spirit of God which assures him of his relation to God, yet the abuse of this doctrine should not prevent the logical and scriptural use of it. This testimony is a kind of demonstration, or evidence, superior to those that come to us merely through theological or educational advantages. It is an evidence unknown to the wisest philosopher or scholar, for it comes not through intellectual training, or superior learning along philosophic and scientific lines, but comes by divine revelation, and its author is God. It is a lively apprehension wrought upon the spiritual intuitions of the soul, by which, through the illumination of the Spirit, we are able to grasp the reality of spiritual truth and experience. The witness of the Spirit, because of its very nature, must ever be shrouded in a degree of mystery to any who do not possess it. Dr. Daniel Steele says, "The soul has a set of spiritual intuitions which become active under the illumination of the Spirit. These intuitions are the basis of all real spiritual knowledge. The truths of the Bible are not real to the soul until they have been made real by the *Spirit* of truth."

The witness of our spirit, or the indirect witness, is to be seen in that we do know the work has taken place because of visible and conscious changes that have come into our lives. The Word points to various evidences or results of being born again; we look into our hearts in search of those evidences; if we possess them we may logically, Scripturally and reasonably announce that the work is done. For instance, the

Word declares that "He that is born of God doth not commit sin." All right. Do you commit sin? If so, you have substantial proof that you are not born of God. The Word declares, "This is the love of God, that we keep his commandments" (1 Jno. 5:3), and "He that keepeth his commandments dwelleth in him" (1 Jno. 3:24). All right. Do you keep His commandments? If not, then you may reasonably know that you are not dwelling in him, and that you have not the love of God in you, for the Book declares, "He that hath my commandments, and keepeth them, *he it is that loveth me*" (Jno. 14:21). The Word declares, "We know that we have passed from death unto life because we love the brethren." All right. Do you harbor ill will, grudge, malice, jealousy or hatred? If you do you may well know that you have not passed from death unto life. The Book says, "Every branch in me that beareth not fruit, he taketh it away." All right. Are you bearing fruit as a Christian? If your life is fruitless, you may well know that you are not a living branch in the vine.

It is folly to assume that you may have the blessing of sanctification, and be minus the fruits of the sanctified life; just as much as it is absurd to profess the grace of regeneration, without measuring up to the quality of the life of a regenerated soul. But what are the fruits of a sanctified life? The outstanding evidences we believe are, fullness of the Spirit, power for service and purity of heart (Acts 2:4; Acts 1:8; Acts 15:9). Have you these evidences? Are you filled with the Spirit; have you Holy Spirit power for service for your Lord; and are you cleansed from all sin? It ought not to be a difficult matter to determine the witness of our own spirit to these matters. If our own spirit can witness to these evidences of sanctification, and God's Spirit gives us an inward assurance, or conviction, corresponding to our own; we may rest assured that we have a scriptural, logical and reasonable evidence that will pass muster any time or any place, regardless of our physical or emotional feelings.

To sum the whole matter up, the scriptural evidence of sanctification is an inward assurance wrought by the Holy Ghost upon the intuitions of the soul, convincing us of His faithfulness in bringing to pass what he has promised, upon the basis of our having complied with the conditions laid down in His Word for the reception of such things; plus the witness of our own spirit which is conscious of such work being accomplished, by the fruits of a divine transformation having taken place within us. Any man who applies these spiritual marks, may know he is either saved or sanctified, as literally as he may know whether he is married or single, drunk or sober, sick or well, or whether he is honorable or disreputable.

CHAPTER XIV

CATECHETICAL APPENDIX

QUESTION 1. *Does sanctification remove temptation?*

ANSWER. Sanctification, or holiness, never implies anything more nor less than the being saved from all sin. Jesus was holy, harmless, undefiled and separate from sinners (Heb. 7:26), but was in all points tempted like as we are, yet without sin (Heb. 4:15). In order to remove man from the possibility of temptation, it would be necessary to remove from him the God given endowment of free moral agency. God never takes away from man anything in sanctification but sin; He never takes away from man by grace anything that He originally gave him in creation. Thus man is a free moral agent and as such is ever susceptible to temptation and the possibility of sinning. There are different orders of holy beings, but all alike have been subject to temptation. Adam in his Edenic state, Jesus upon the "exceeding high mountain," and the angels who kept not their first estate were all tempted.

No doubt the motive in the mind of the infinite Creator was, by this method, to prove the quality of our integrity. Virtue, in order to be virtue, must be the product of our own volitional choice. Integrity and fidelity can only be such when it has been the result of exercising our own prerogative. An act to deserve merit or reward must be the product of our preference and choice. There is no virtue in goodness that *could not* have done otherwise, and there is no responsibility where an act was unavoidable. The real quality of our conduct is based upon our free moral agency, in our ability and preference to choose right and reject wrong. To take away from us the possibility of temptation, would likewise remove the matter of merit or demerit, and thus deprive us of rewards or retribution.

"Moral excellency," says Rev. Asbury Lowery, D. D., "becomes more conspicuous, bright and beautiful when it has passed through the ordeal of solicitation and comes out untainted. Spiritual goodness, moral integrity and purpose of character are all confirmed and solidified in the degree that they cleave to the right and renounce the wrong. In fact, Christian character, like gold and silver, is refined in the crucible of temptation and testing. The place to test the soldier is not on dress parade when the crowd is cheering and the bands are playing and flags are flying, but on the battle field and in the siege of conflict and deprivation. Here is the place to display courage and fortitude, sacrifice and determination that can win battles."

Yes, the sanctified soul is susceptible to temptation, and as one writer very suggestively says, "Temptation is to the soul's integrity what calisthenics are to the physical body. The hours that are spent in temptation are like the hours spent in a gymnasium to the physical man. If God is to have healthy, well developed spiritual beings, He must develop them through the exercise of their moral powers of choice. Though the hours of temptation may be unpleasant and the conflict desperate, nevertheless these are the times of our greatest development and progress in the realms of grace" (1 Peter 1:6, 7). Severe temptations produce a tenderness and kindness for others, a degree of humility and love, a sympathy and patience, for our fellow-men that is often sadly lacking in some who profess very high standards of grace. He can best sympathize with the tempted and tried who has himself been through the fires of severe testing (Heb. 2:18).

QUESTION 2. *Is it necessary to call it sanctification?*

ANSWER. It is surprising to see how many people would like to enjoy this experience and have this great grace, but who are unwilling to suffer the reproach that goes with it (Heb. 13:12, 13). There has always been a peculiar sense of embarrassment that accompanies true piety, in a world that has always been unfriendly to grace, but this is especially so relative to sanctification. We are not a stickler for terms. We have often heard the experience referred to by other names; we are not dogmatic, or contentious in this matter, except that we believe it is best to stick to Scriptural phraseology, and not attempt to be wise above what is written. Jesus once said, "Whosoever therefore shall be ashamed of me *and of my words* in this adulterous and sinful generation, of him also shall the Son of man be ashamed, when he cometh in the glory of his Father with the holy angels" (Mark 8:38). It seems to the writer that dodging Scriptural terms is simply an effort to make the doctrine palatable in the eyes of its antagonists; an effort to take away the reproach that accompanies this experience. To say the least it is certainly misleading to call anything by a wrong name. If a parent should desire a rose from his garden and say to his child, "Bring me a flower," never specifying what kind of a flower, he would be just as likely to get any other kind as he would a rose. The man who uses such indefinite and comprehensive terms relative to this matter is so indefinite that he will likely get nothing definite. Yes, it is best to call it sanctification; best to call it what God calls it; best to use Scriptural phraseology.

QUESTION 3. *What is the difference in the love of a sanctified and a regenerated man; does God give an imperfect love to the converted?*

ANSWER. God gives no faulty love to anybody. He gives His love to those who are saved, and we do not question the quality of that love. We do not believe that God gives imperfect love to His children. Then the reader may ask, "Why then do you make the distinction of love and perfect love in the regenerated and sanctified person?" The imperfectness of the love in the regenerated man's heart is not due to lack of the quality of love given him, but due to its inability to function perfectly, owing to an antagonistic element in his nature which seeks to hinder it in the exercise of its constitutional functions. God gives the proper quality of love always to all His people, but love that is hindered by carnality in the exercise of its constitutional functions is imperfect, not because of the quality of love that God gave, but because of the antagonistic element within the heart of the justified man that seeks to hinder its operation. The removal of this antagonistic element (inbred sin) from the heart of the justified man, through sanctification, now enables this love to function properly and according to the standard of perfect love.

QUESTION 4. *Does the regenerated man have the Holy Spirit?*

ANSWER. Some say that the Holy Spirit will not take up His abode in a heart that is not fully sanctified, therefore the regenerated man must be holy, or he does not possess the Holy Spirit. We do not think the Holy Spirit will dwell in a heart where there is conscious disobedience to God. If there is conscious disobedience to God, however, such soul *is not* justified. There should no doubt be a distinction between actual sin and inbred sin. One involves guilt and condemnation, for it has to do with our free moral agency; the other is birth sin, and involves no personal responsibility for its presence in the heart until such time as the individual may receive light upon its presence and the manner of his deliverance. A refusal to walk in keeping with the light upon this matter will bring condemnation, as disobedience always does, and the Holy Spirit lives in no heart that is condemned. That individual, however, who has been born of the Spirit of God, made a partaker of the divine nature and is walking in all the light he has, and is keeping step with God, has the Spirit, for, "If any man have not the Spirit of Christ, he is none of his" (Rom. 8:9). We who are converted doubtless have received the "Spirit of adoption, whereby we cry, Abba, Father" (Rom 8:14, 15).

To take away the privilege of having the Spirit in the converted life, would be to take away all that is divine and supernatural in regeneration, and leave the converted man with nothing more than a mere human religion, that consists of only a reformation. The man that is born of the Spirit certainly has the Holy Spirit; but sanctification, no doubt gives to him the Spirit in fullness of measure and in a different sense from that which he knew in regeneration, as may be seen from such scriptures as Acts 2:4; Eph. 3:19; Jno. 14:15, 17; Eph. 4:11, 13, and others. Let the reader not be satisfied until he has received the "*fullness* of the blessing of the gospel of Christ."

QUESTION 5. *Why are the children of holy parentage not born holy?*

ANSWER. Holiness is a bestowment of divine grace; it is the gift of God; it is an acquired moral quality through faith, and must always be received this way, as it cannot be transmitted by the natural order of generation. Dr. John R. Brooks very clearly answers this question when he says, "Does not what scientists call the law of reversion to type," which runs through the vegetable and animal kingdom, explain the fact? Take a simple example where this reversion is immediate. By grafting the crab with the pippin we greatly improve the fruit of the tree, bringing it to comparative perfection. But from the seed of the pippin will spring the crab, which will never bear good fruit until it in turn is grafted from the superior tree. So the man that by being grafted into Christ bears the sweet, luscious fruit of perfect love can never impart this nature to his children. They will revert to the original type of depraved human nature, and will themselves have to be grafted into Christ before they can bring forth the fruit borne by their parents."

QUESTION 6. *Can a man lose his sanctification, and not lose his justification?*

ANSWER. The principal error in assuming that one can be lost and not the other, is, we believe, in the failure to discriminate between the joy of this experience and the experience itself. Notwithstanding the joy of sanctification may not always be so pronounced, the absence of this joy is not always indicative of the fact that one has lost the grace of a pure heart. It is possible for a person to be in heaviness for various reasons other than sin. Through manifold temptation, physical infirmities and other causes the soul may be in a spirit of heaviness, be discouraged and under a cloud without becoming carnal again. We take it that if there is no conscious knowledge of wilful disobedience to God you have forfeited neither your sanctification nor your justification. If there is a knowledge of your disobedience to Him, you have forfeited both.

In order to lose sanctification, we must become carnal again, otherwise, so long as our heart remains pure we are sanctified. God's law relative to sin we believe to be immutable; it never changes and if this is so we may reasonably conclude that whatever it took to originally make men carnal it will take the same today. What was the law of . God relative to this matter; how did man originally become carnal? By transgression. If the law of God is unchangeable, how is he to become carnal again? By transgression. In the original forfeiture of our holiness, when man transgressed God's law, did he lose only his holiness, or did he lose both? As a matter of sacred record, did he not forfeit both the divine image and also spiritual life, and become a sinner dead in trespasses and sins? If transgression originally caused a forfeiture of heart purity, and produced spiritual death; why need we expect it to do less today? Where there is conscious disobedience to God, there can be no justification nor sanctification. Where there is *no* conscious disobedience to God, you retain both. Where there is no disobedience to the point of condemnation we should never cast away our confidence and be swindled out of our experience because of temptations, or heaviness for other causes, for until you have disobeyed wilfully and knowingly, you have forfeited nothing; while if you have disobeyed wilfully and knowingly, you should not try to make yourself believe you are a Christian at all. In a word, so long as you have been guilty of no known transgression of God's law you have lost no work of grace; but if you are guilty of knowingly transgressing God's law you have lost your justification as well as your sanctification, for disobedience and justification are incompatible terms. It is a contradiction to say that you disobeyed God and are justified; while if you have not disobeyed Him, you have no reason to assume you have lost your sanctification.

There may be times of heaviness and sorrow in the sanctified life, but unless these have been brought on because of your wilful disobedience, it is folly to assert that you have lost your sanctification. The Ohio River is just as much the Ohio River at low water time as when it is overflowing its banks; and the soul that is going through a dry place, a hard time and difficult problems is just as much sanctified as when he is shouting happy, if there has been no conscious disobedience to God. If there is a consciousness of our disobedience to Him, we might as well tell the truth, come clean and confess that we are backslidden.

The writer has not overlooked the fact that many talk about their sanctification *leaking out*, but still retaining their justification. Upon close analysis it will likely be found that when the hole is discovered through which their sanctification leaked away, it was so large that their justification also ran out, and that such hole was the product of disobedience. Yes, one may lose the joy and exuberance, the emotional happiness, without losing the experience itself; but when the situation has become so serious as to forfeit your heart purity and become carnal again it is more than likely that justification went with it. What kind of transgression would it be that would lose sanctification and not lose justification. Is it not more than likely that an offense so serious as to cause us to forfeit this great experience would make us feel bad and put us under condemnation? Very well, "There is therefore now no condemnation to them that are in Christ Jesus." An offense therefore that brings upon the soul a sense of guilt and condemnation is of sufficient magnitude to not only cause a forfeiture of sanctification, but justification as well. Cast not away your confidence if you have not sinned; do not let Satan rob you of your blood bought experience; it is yours *as long as you obey Him*. If you have sinned, ask God to forgive you; again consecrate yourself to Him and trust Him to restore to you pardoning love and cleansing power. Taking all the facts into consideration, if you have sinned, you have forfeited justification as well as sanctification for justification is incompatible with sin; if you have not sinned wilfully and knowingly, you have forfeited neither justification nor sanctification.

QUESTION 7. *Is it instantaneous or progressive?*

ANSWER. Without going into detail of technicalities, we would say it is both. Sanctification in its relation to cleansing is instantaneous; wrought by the Holy Ghost, through consecration and faith. Sanctification as it relates to the development and building of Christian character is progressive. No reputable teacher of the doctrine of sanctification teaches that sanctification is maturity in spiritual things; in fact any grace, or degree of grace, ought to be progressive. Regeneration is an instantaneous work so far as the work of a supernatural transformation is concerned; but the regenerated man finds himself far away from the place of his instantaneous conversion after he has walked with God several months. Likewise, the soul who sought and found this wonderful experience of sanctification will find that while the matter of this wonderful cleansing baptism was an instantaneous work, as he has kept step with God and walked in the light he has made great and rapid progress in the things of sanctification.

There are some who would make the cleansing from all sin to be progressive, as for instance, they say that the apostle's prayer to be entirely (or wholly) sanctified is to be unto the coming (or at the coming) of our Lord Jesus Christ. Therefore this sanctification is gradual, that is, coming to completion at the coming of the Lord. One certainly has considerable rubber in this theological thinking, and unlimited powers of imagination, to stretch this cleansing over an entire lifetime. The very fact that the apostle says, "And preserve you blameless unto [or at, as they prefer to interpret it] the coming of the Lord Jesus Christ," suggests that the work is a finished work. The word preserved (that is, kept) itself involves the quality of time and infers that the work is done instantaneously and that we are to be preserved (or kept) in that state unto the coming of the Lord. We could not well be kept in an experience that we were not yet possessing. The progressive cleansers also cite us to Heb. 2:11, which says, "Both he that sanctifieth and they who are sanctified are all of one, for which cause he is not ashamed to call them brethren." They say that the translation "they who are sanctified" should read "they who are *being sanctified*." Granting that some translations may read this way, it would require a considerable stretch of our imagination to imply that such language indicated a long drawn out course of procedure. The writer might say that we are adding to the church such as are *being converted,* but that in nowise indicates that the matter of their conversion is a progressive conversion, spreading over their entire lifetime; yet it would be just as reasonable to say that *"being converted"* indicated a gradual or progressive conversion as to say that *"being sanctified"* signified a long drawn out progressive affair, that took it beyond the place of any present tense value. We conclude that sanctification, as it relates to the cleansing of the soul from sin, is instantaneous; as it relates to development or maturity of Christian character, it is progressive.

QUESTION 8. *Do the best people agree with this teaching?*

ANSWER. This is by no means a modern question. "Have any of the rulers believed on him?" was the question they were asking in the day of Jesus and His disciples. The truth of God's Word is not dependent upon the endorsement of any set of people. If, therefore, the Word of the Lord establishes and confirms this truth, it needs not the endorsement of men to make it true. The writer has lived long enough to know that sometimes very intelligent people can be mistaken; and that sometimes even the higher ups go wrong. Any person whose doctrine does not conform to this wonderful Word is wrong. If it is the bishop, or dean of theology, or the eloquent doctor of divinity that is in error; he is just as much in error as an unlearned peasant. The best people also are not always, necessarily, the rich, the educated, and the socially influential from the standpoint of the opinions of the world.

Weak, fickle humanity is always wanting to be popular and to be with the majority. John says, "Nevertheless among the chief rulers also, many believed on him; but because of the Pharisees, they did not confess him, lest they should be put out of the synagogue." It would be well indeed if we were as much concerned about being right as we are about being popular. The answer to the question, however, depends on what is being implied by the best people. If by the best people we mean those who are high in authority, in social life, or ranking high financially, the answer would be one thing; if you mean by the best people, those who are noted for their high moral integrity and deep spiritual insight, it would be another. Popular opinion is not the source of authority on spiritual matters; so let us stick to the Word, regardless of what others believe. Public opinion on this matter may be seen by referring to the chapter in this book entitled, "The Voice of the Ecclesia."